THE SOCIAL ORGANIZATION OF THE MARRI BALUCH

VIKING FUND PUBLICATIONS IN ANTHROPOLOGY

Number Forty-Three

THE

SOCIAL ORGANIZATION

OF THE

MARRI BALUCH

by ROBERT N. PEHRSON

compiled and analyzed from his notes

by FREDRIK BARTH

Subscriber's edition

distributed through

CURRENT ANTHROPOLOGY

for the

WENNER-GREN FOUNDATION FOR ANTHROPOLOGICAL RESEARCH, INCORPORATED

1966

This volume comprises one of a series of publications on research in general anthropology published by the Wenner-Gren Foundation for Anthropological Research, Incorporated, a foundation created and endowed at the instance of Axel L. Wenner-Gren for scientific, educational, and charitable purposes. The reports, numbered consecutively as independent contributions, appear at irregular intervals.

Edited by SOL TAX, University of Chicago

TO *Jean*

for her work, courage, and faithfulness

PREFACE

THIS MONOGRAPH attempts to analyze and present the results of anthropological fieldwork done among the Marri Baluch by Robert N. Pehrson and
his wife, Jean Pehrson. The Pehrsons arrived in Pakistan in November,
1954, and started their fieldwork by mid-December in a village in the Marri area
of Baluchistan. From March, 1955, they lived and migrated with various camps of
Marri nomads until Robert Pehrson's death after a short illness on September 8,
1955.

In the course of this period they learned to speak Baluchi with considerable
fluency and succeeded in establishing very close relations with the members of
several tent camps. They were encouraged to use Marri dress and adopted the
style of life appropriate to the sex of each, she running a native household and
participating in the activities of the women, he acting as the head of the household, working with the men, and increasingly entering into the life of the communities in which he resided.

Perhaps he ran unnecessary risks by taking our teachers' standards of participation more literally than they themselves have done. The barren campsites on
vast and desolate plains and mountains which shepherds pointed out to me as his,
with three rocks for the griddle on which his wife baked their unleavened bread
and miles of rough ground to the nearest pool of dirty and brackish water, bear
witness of a life of stark austerity in pursuit of full participation. Yet the very
bleakness of Marri life was no doubt both a challenge and a satisfaction to him.

His time among the Marri was not altogether a happy one. The hollowness of
much Marri etiquette and the deceit of their intimate life disturbed him. In this
respect the unassuming reserve of the Lapps, whom he had loved so much, was
probably far more congenial to him personally. Yet he dedicated himself to
"becoming a Marri" as he had earlier become a Lapp, and in the schizoid condition of participant field-work he must have sensed toward the end that he had
finally succeeded in crossing a boundary and partly entering into a new culture.
His death on the ground in that small Marri encampment consummated this
success; Marris have erected a cairn on the spot where he died and visit the
place occasionally to make a sacrifice.

From his notes it has been only partly possible to retrace his intellectual journey. In attempting it, I have had the dual purpose of honoring his memory and salvaging what seemed of most value in a masterly but uncompleted field-work. I do not think our discipline has any need for a cult of the dead as martyrs or saints, but as his friend and colleague I should like Robert Pehrson to be recognized and remembered for what he achieved in his short career as an anthropologist. And for the anthropological study of Middle Eastern societies I believe his material is of a value to justify fully the time and effort that have gone into its analysis and presentation for publication.

For the orientation of the reader, I will summarize briefly the events surround-ing the fieldwork and analysis that have resulted in the present manuscript. Such a summary may be of use in two ways. It gives a basis for judging the reliability of the data and the adequacy of the analysis. Moreover, because the observations were made by one person and the task of analysis was mainly performed by another, these two phases of work are distinguishable in a way that is unusual in social anthropology and this invites some methodological reflections that may be of more general interest.

Robert Pehrson formulated his research scheme in the course of the autumn of 1953, basing it mainly on his previous experience with Lappish reindeer nomads and the inadequate published ethnographies of peoples of the Afghan-Pakistan area. His focus of interest was the relationship between social structure and ecology among pastoral nomads. He obtained support from the Ford Foundation for a three-year program of study, including a one-year intensive field study of a single group and a further year's fieldwork (after an intervening period of analysis) among other nomadic and sedentary groups in a larger region. After some doubt he decided that Baluchistan offered the best opportunities for field-work. The Marri tribe was elected for the first intensive field study only after his arrival in Pakistan, in consultation with Pakistani authorities.

He and hs wife, who was trained as a philosopher, arrived in Karachi in November, 1954, as I was leaving after completing fieldwork among Pathans, and we were together for three days, discussing our plans and materials. By Christmas they had established themselves in a large sedentary village in the Marri area, where they spent three months learning the language and collecting material on the community. Subsequently, they spent more than five months living and moving with Marri nomadic camps, their longest residence being with the camp referred to in the text as "Mir's camp," where Robert Pehrson died on September 8, 1955.

They both felt that fieldwork had been very difficult and slow. The material from the village is rich but incomplete. The camps they had lived with showed great structural variation, and they were greatly impressed by the complexity of the area as well as discouraged by the difficulties and suspicions they constantly met with in their work. The last two months, however, were highly productive of sound data, which they finally believed were adequate and reliable for analytical purposes.

At the point at which it was interrupted, their joint work had provided rich material on kinship, domestic organization, and camps. On political organization and, perhaps surprisingly, ecology the data were much thinner and poorer. They were planning to turn increasingly to problems of tribal politics in the last part of their first year's work, but the ecological interrelations of groups appeared unexpectedly complex and would require, they thought, the perspective of a second, regionally and comparatively oriented, field year for their elucidation.

The two of them tried, as much as possible, to duplicate data, each from the sphere of his or her own sex. The complexity and richness of the data, especially on kinship and domestic life, derive from this effort. On some topics, such as formal law and politics, there was no overlap, since these matters did not interest the women, and the situations in which most data were collected differed markedly, in that he obtained most from formal and informal gatherings of men in which they explained, discussed, or decided on matters, whereas she obtained most of her material from private commentary, direct observation, and eavesdropping.

No analyses of any part of the material had been written down, though some interpretation and even discussion was occasionally incorporated into the day-by-day notes. During their fieldwork, we also maintained an intermittent correspondence, so I have about half a dozen letters describing and discussing select points and problems as they appeared to Bob Pehrson at the time.

In due course Jean Pehrson typed up the field notes (a total of about 200 pages), as well as texts of stories and poetry and copies of their private correspondence from the field. Because of the assumed affinity between Baluch and Pathan cultures, and considerable similarities in the professional interests and views of Pehrson and myself, as well as for personal reasons, I agreed to analyze and edit these notes for publication. Later I had made available to me two manuscripts by Jean Pehrson: a sixty-page essay on Marri values—an extremely insightful analysis of ethics and behavior, on which I have relied heavily—and a brief sketch of leadership in Marri society.

My repeated attempts at writing up this material were most frustrating. Lacking any kind of connected analysis from Robert Pehrson's hand, I found it impossible to work systematically with the notes; all attempts at creating a taxonomy of "the parts of Marri culture" were defeated by the diversity of the data. I proceeded to learn the total mass of data—to memorize it all, in the hope that an overall *Gestalt* would then be revealed. I finally decided that the failure might be caused by the lack of adequate political and ecological data and that in any case the only hope of success lay in being able myself to visit the area.

I was able to combine such a plan with a visit to West Pakistan for my own fieldwork purposes, and the Wenner-Gren Foundation very graciously supported the project. In the autumn of 1960 I was therefore able to spend some five weeks in the Marri area, with the main purpose of filling some lacunae in the material and of obtaining a concrete "feel" for the society and culture in question. A number of factors combined to make this visit singularly successful; local administrators of the lower echelons had known, or heard of, Bob Pehrson and went to great lengths to facilitate my work in every way. Marri chiefs similarly vied at being ready to help me. And, very fortunately, all the camps in which the Pehrsons had worked contained persons knowledgable in Pashto, while in "Mir's camp" both men and women were practically bilingual in Pashto and Baluchi, thereby making it possible for me to communicate freely with them on the basis of my previous knowledge of Pashto.

I committed the inaccuracy of introducing myself as Robert Pehrson's classificatory brother, and the Marri were deeply moved by the idea of my coming from so far away to see the people among whom he had lived his last year. They showered on me all the goodwill that he had so laboriously accumulated, even incorporating me into the kinship position he had obtained in "Mir's camp" by being marriage brother at a wedding, thus giving me free access to speak with the women of that camp, where I was taken by the camp mistress on the first night to sit like a returned son with her by the women's campfire. At the same time, during the days on horseback traveling through the harsh and desolate landscape seeking the camp groups with which he had lived, I was met with suspicion and deceived by false information, and so had a taste of the other side of Marri life as well.

Returning to the analysis after this brief field experience, I found the material much more tractable. Not only were some previously identified lacunae filled, in a sketchy way, but clearly I had also accumulated data of other kinds, which were not recorded in the Pehrsons' notes but which are needed in anthropological analysis. Yet those notes had seemed adequately complete in most obvious respects, such as in their identification of persons and their attention to extended cases and the circumstances surrounding events, as well as commentaries and generalizations made by informants, and my own Marri notes do not appear to differ significantly in the kind of data they contain. This suggests that there may be kinds of information that are in fact vital to the task of anthropological analysis but that are fairly consistently excluded from our field notes—in other words that we have conventional criteria for identifying observations as data that are inappropriate for the kinds of hypotheses and theories we wish to develop in our analysis. The frequent assertion that anthropology is an art as well as a science might depend precisely on the unsystematic or unreflecting way in which we accumulate part of our basic data.

Despite the experience of having attempted an analysis purely from the data contained in professional field notes, and then subsequently having had the opportunity of supplementing these data by direct observation, it is singularly difficult to identify the critical supplementary data. I believe, however, that they are mainly connected with the concrete "stage" or setting in which social life takes place: the sizes of habitations, the uses of space, the physical as well as the conventional opportunities for communication. Only with a rather complete background of this kind can one evaluate actions in terms of the genuine alternatives of behavior—concretely, what the actor in a case did *not* choose to do, though it had been possible. The interpretation of actions, both in a strategic means-ends perspective and as messages or communication, depends on this knowledge, and case material remains highly ambiguous when it is lacking. Similarly, such knowledge is used to connect behavior patterns of a generalized kind with such cultural abstractions as values and meanings, and customary behavior remains exotic and arbitrary until these connections have been made.

Obviously, the anthropologist in the field does consciously collect such information, but he rarely notes it down very fully and does, I suspect, depend heavily on "feel" in his use of it during interpretation. When little of this information is formally recorded, that probably also depends on the inadequacy or, in part, complete absence of concepts and techniques for notation of such data. That such a makeshift procedure is a serious methodological weakness should hardly need to be stated.

For the final analysis, I have attempted to give the material unity by focusing on the organization and maintenance of camps, because most of the data could be related to this theme. Though trying to present the material so that it would be descriptively cumulative and lead progressively into this analysis, it was not feasible, nor did I feel that it would be defensible, to harness the whole material to it. Consequently, I have written up the material block by block, going through the complete notes each time and marking all information relevant, for example, to kinship, working up a classification under subtopics and a crude index, and completing the kinship chapter before going through the whole process again for the next topic. As a result, the different chapters may be in part disconnected, but some of the dangers of analytic bias are avoided. An unfortunate side effect is the very slow progression of the text, whereby the earlier three or four chapters suffer from a lack of depth in analysis.

Throughout the writing, I have tried to use the formulations of data found in the notes and to intersperse the text as much as possible with verbatim informants' statements—not in an attempt at documentation so much as to constrain my own presentation to stay as close as possible to the implicit views contained in the notes. Finally, Jean Pehrson has checked the whole manuscript both for the data and for the interpretations that it contains.

Despite these attempts, the question can legitimately be raised as to what extent this text as it stands should be regarded as the work of Robert Pehrson. Though the main steps of the analysis have been chosen by me, I have felt throughout that I have done so in a capacity as his colleague and replacement, within a professional tradition of scholarship which we shared. The material, through the data and observations it provides, sets clear limits on choice and positively invites certain lines of analysis. In the kinship chapter I have felt justified in making some use of the formal schema of componential analysis, since Pehrson's own analytical efforts in Lappish kinship (Pehrson, 1957) have an early affinity to this later development. When in a subsequent chapter I pursue a "generative" analysis of camp composition that is logically somewhat reminiscent of this, I do so not so much because such analyses interest me at the moment as because it seemed the most adequate way of handling the problem and did not appear unrelated to his own way of thinking as exemplified, for example, in his article on the Lappish herding leader (Pehrson, 1954). I have no doubt that, had he been allowed to continue, he would have carried his analysis further, and partly along different lines from the ones I have been able to suggest. I am also aware that every statement in the text of necessity bears my mark as well as his. But I have seriously endeavored—and I think largely succeeded in the effort— to give a picture of Marri social organization that derives entirely from his work and that is substantively very close to that which he himself would have given on the basis of the material he had at his command by September, 1955.

FREDRIK BARTH

CONTENTS

THE SOCIAL ORGANIZATION OF THE MARRI BALUCH

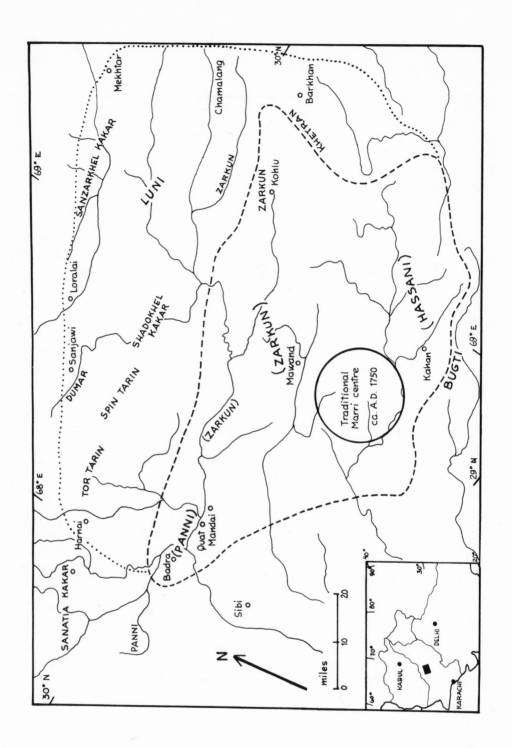

I

GEOGRAPHY AND HISTORY

THE MARRI BALUCH tribal area lies in northeastern Baluchistan, West Pakistan, and comprises a tangled mass of precipitous mountains and ridges separating flat valley bottoms filled with rock and alluvium. The general trend of the ridges, produced by the tilting of limestone beds, is east-west, but the main slope of the land is from north to south, producing a complex and erratic drainage pattern mainly debouching toward the southwest. Communications are extremely difficult between the valleys, since passes negotiable even by horse are few and widely separated. The valley bottoms lie at 2,000–3,000 feet, and the highest peak is more than 8,000 feet above sea level (*Baluchistan District Gazetteer*, III [1907], 264-65).

The climate is hot and dry, with considerable seasonal fluctuation. Through most of the area the temperature varies from below freezing in the winter to 130° F. in the summer. Annual rainfall is about five inches, subject to much local and annual variation, and falls mainly in two seasons, as winter rain and as summer monsoon. However, except perhaps in the northwest corner of the Marri area, the effect of the winter rain is relatively negligible, and the Marris themselves generally consider their two periods of precipitation to fall at the close of spring and, mainly, at the close of summer. Particularly at that time, in August and September, storms strike suddenly and violently, with thunder and lightning and windstorms and furious duststorms, followed by torrential rains, which create flash floods in riverbeds that are normally dry ten months of the year. Perennial streams and waterholes, on the other hand, are few.

Under such circumstances vegetation is sparse, and the landscape presents a barren and desolate aspect. River courses tend to be lined with low stands of thorny trees, a few places extending across the valley bottom, and some of the hillsides have some scrub cover, though most are completely barren. A characteristic feature is the frequent occurrence of colonies of dwarf palm, providing flecks of deep green in an otherwise buff, brown, and black landscape. From late spring into summer, however, the country experiences a florescence, with brightly colored flowering trees and shrubs and a sparse stand of herbs and grasses.

1

The area delimited on the map as "Marri Tribal Area" comprises 3,268 square miles and constitutes a separate administrative unit within which tribal Marri administration and law are recognized. A certain number of the nearly 60,000 Marris, however, live outside this area in Duki, Sanjawi, Barkhan, and Sibi Tahsils, while retaining their tribal rights, whereas few non-Marris live permanently within the Marri area. A rough estimate of the population density might therefore be fifteen persons per square mile.

The Marri area lies in the extreme northeast of the land at present occupied by Baluchis. On the north it borders on the territory of Kakar and Luni Pathans—an area also visited in the winter by Afghan Powindah pastoral nomads. To the east are the Khetrans, who speak a dialect peculiar to themselves but akin to Sindhi and Jatki (Dames 1904: 16). To the south are the Bugti Baluchis, who are closely similar to the Marris and are their traditional enemies. To the west the Marri adjoin the non-tribal districts of the Sibi basin, inhabited by a mixed population speaking Sindhi, Baluchi, or Pashto. The Marri and Bugti, together with a few Baluch tribes in the Indus Valley, are further separated from the main body of Baluch by the Dravidian-speaking Brahui tribes of Kalat, and this separation correlates with a clear dialect difference between the northeastern tribes and the central Baluch tribes of Mekran and Chagai. The Baluchi language belongs, together with Persian and Kurdish, to the western branch of the Iranian language family.

An authoritative traditional view of Baluch history, as it affects the northeastern tribes in particular, is given by Dames (1904) and will be summarized briefly. The linguistic connections suggest a westerly ethnic origin, and Arab sources of about A.D. 1000 indicate Kerman as the homeland of the Baluchis at that time (pp. 29 ff.). Oral traditions describe an invasion and residence in Sistan before the descent on Mekran and the Sindh frontier (pp. 33 ff.). Then, about A.D. 1500, the first great invasion of India took place, under the leadership of Mir Chakur Rind (pp. 39 ff.), resulting in the conquest and looting of much of northwestern India and the permanent occupation of Multan and other districts of South Panjab. The exploits of Mir Chakur and his warriors form the favorite topic of northern Baluchi legendary ballads, but few of the tribes mentioned persist today as organized groups, and tribes like the Marri do not appear in the accounts. The Baluchis themselves say that "those who followed Chakur have become Jatts, while those who stayed behind have remained Baloches" (p. 48).

The present Marri area appears subsequently to have been occupied by Rinds of the Gorgezh and Kalmati tribes and by Buledhis of a separate Baluch stem, all three of whom fought over the land. A song attributed to the Gorgezh characterizes the period:

The mountains are the Baloches' forts; these hills are better than an army. The lofty heights are our comrades, the pathless gorges our friends. Our drink is from the flowing springs, our cups the leaf of the dwarf-palm, our beds the thorny brush, the ground our pillow. My horse is my white sandals. For my sons you may take the arrows, for my brethren the broad shield, for my father the wide-wounding sword [pp.49–50].

The Gorgezh succeeded in evicting the Buledhis but later lost the land to the Kalmatis and persist only as a small fragment at Thali near Sibi. The Kalmatis were succeeded by the Hasanis—Baluchi-speakers but perhaps of Pathan origin (p. 58)—who were finally evicted about 1830 after protracted struggles by a combination of the Marris and Bugtis. Hasanis now live scattered in the area, as well as in an organized group among the Khetrans (p. 50). As for the Marri themselves, Dames notes in his list of politically organized Baluch tribes, that they are

one of the best known among Baluch tribes for their marauding propensities. Of composite origin. The Ghazani section are supposed to be descended from Ghazan, son of Ali, son of Jalal Khan, and the Bijeranis from Bijar, who revolted against Mir Chakur. The Mazaranis are said to be of Khetran origin, and the Loharanis of mixed descent. No doubt some Jatts, and also some Kalmatis, Buledhis and Hasanis have been absorbed, and perhaps some Pathan elements also among the Bijaranis [p. 5].

What defines and delimits the Marri as a social unit is thus, not common origin and descent, but political identity as an organized *tuman*, or politically independent tribe (pp. 3 ff.). The critical office in this tribal organization is that of the central chief, the *tumandar* or *sardar*. There is reason to believe that the role of the sardar, and the functions of the whole tribal apparatus of organization, have changed radically over the last hundred years. At its inception, Marri tribal organization may have been primarily an organization of fighting men for military expeditions and the division of spoils. Robbery and looting were clearly a major activity in what was then one of Asia's most unsettled areas (cf. early travelers and frontier officers, such as Pottinger, Ferrier, Mason, Holdich, Bruce), and it was indeed only by defeating other groups in war that the different segments that today form the Marri tribe were able to obtain the present Marri area. The political climate was one of violence and anarchy. One informant says:

"In my father's time, there was nothing but fighting—the slashing of swords, the banging of guns. My father had a sword cut in his right shoulder and on his arms, and was hit in the thigh by a bullet. That was the whole story in those days—bang bang, slash slash." [1]

During the first period of contact with the Marri-Bugti, the British administration in Sindh offered its native troops a reward of R. 10/- for each tribesman, upon delivery to a British horseman (*Frontier and Overseas Expeditions from*

1. Statements by Marri informants as reproduced in Pehrson's notes, are indicated throughout the book by quotation marks, without accompanying reference.

India, III, 89), and Bruce (1900) cites an incident in which, to the officer's em-
barrassment, one of the men claiming his reward produced the severed head of
a tribesman as evidence, in the presence of one of the British ladies.

With the institution of Sandeman's "Forward Policy" of active indirect rule,
conditions changed rapidly (Bruce 1900), and the last battle fought by the
Marri tribe was at Gumbaz in 1918. Today, the main concern of the tribal councils is with the settlement of disputes on the basis of custom law; the area is
comparatively quiet, and cooperation with external authorities is so close that,
for practical purposes, the apex of Marri tribal organization could be said to be
the extra assistant commissioner in charge of Marri-Bugti, rather than the Marri
sardar.

Throughout these changes Marri economy has been based on mixed herding
and agriculture, but population density, residence, and land-use patterns have
changed considerably. Whereas some previous occupants of present Marri territory, such as the Khetrans and Hasanis, were and are village people, the Marri
themselves have been tent-dwellers, as were most of their Baluchi forebears. But
under present conditions the trend is toward larger and more permanent
settlements.

"In the old days there were very few mud villages. The people then lived in mat
tents. Now many villages have been made and also many winter huts have been built."

There may also have been an increased differentiation between nomad and
settled Marri.

"When I was young . . . the Marris moved only a short distance, from this plain
to that mountain and back. There was plenty of room for grazing. Now there is little.
People have increased. Herds have increased. . . . With greater population, more land
is being cultivated. But these days the Marri migrate much more and have moved into
territories not heretofore their own."

In spite of this increased mobility, a great majority of the nomadic households
continue to support themselves in part by agriculture, as well as by herding.
In districts outside the Marri tribal area, such as the much-visited fringe of
Pathan lands to the north, agricultural land is obtained on tenancy contracts or
residence is seasonal and households maintain fields within the Marri area to the
south.

Political and ecologic relations in the Marri area are thus in a state of flux;
synchronically one meets much variation, and there is clear evidence of recent
historical change. The following description focuses particularly on one mode
of contemporary Marri life: that of the nomadic camps, either pastoral or of
mixed economy, which is still the predominant mode of life of the Marri and
also seems the one in which most characteristically Marri features of the culture
find their expression.

II

MARRI SUBSISTENCE AND RESIDENCE FORMS

MARRI SUBSISTENCE is based on the simultaneous exploitation of a number of different ecological niches and characteristically involves the coordination of activities that can only with difficulty be combined. Variable patterns of subsistence and residence emerge through different combinations and compromises between these activities. This chapter describes the different subsistence activities and the patterns that emerge from their different combinations.

Herding. In spite of its arid and inhospitable appearance, the Marri area offers opportunities for a pastoral economy based on various hardy and drought-resistant strains of common domesticated species. The most important are sheep, goats, cattle, donkeys, and dogs; fairly common also are camels, horses, and chickens. Of these animals, only the sheep and goats are significant producers. Cows give very little milk and are kept mainly for reproductive purposes, to provide bullocks for labor and to supplement the bullocks in their work. This work is mainly connected with agriculture, that is, plowing and threshing, but cattle are also utilized during migrations as beasts of burden. More important for this purpose, however, are donkeys, while camels are used for heavy transport, in caravan trade or for carrying produce to market, in construction work, etc. Horses are ridden and constitute important prestige items. Dogs are used for the protection of camps and herds, not actively to control the herds as shepherd dogs.

Marri sheep are small, even compared with those of neighboring people; they are very white with black noses, while the goats are black. The relative value of sheep and goats varies from 2 sheep = 3 goats to 1 sheep = 2 goats. Sheep and, more especially, goats give some milk beyond that required by their lambs and kids, and the Marri churn butter and make cheese or consume the milk directly. They are unwilling to sell any dairy products, however, and there is a widely held idea that if the owner breaks the taboo an animal in his herd will die. The important pastoral products are thus wool and meat. The wool (and goat hair) is cut twice yearly and gives an annual income per animal of about 3–4 rupees. Livestock is also sold for slaughter, and meat is a mainstay of the Marri diet.

Herding activities are controlled by the availability of pasture and water. The grasses that provide the better pasture necessary for cattle and sheep flourish from April into summer; from then on, the herd must subsist on parched fodder, supplemented in the case of the goats by browsing. The donkeys also are able to browse, and even cattle eat twigs and dwarf-palm leaves. Horses are unable to subsist on local pasturage and are provided for by their owners with grass cut from irrigated areas and with grains. Though the plants in the pastures are useful for camels, and could support them, these animals have difficulty covering sufficient areas for their grazing requirements because of the rockiness of the terrain, and their condition tends to deteriorate if they are kept long in most Marri areas. Wealthy men who own camels therefore generally board them with villagers in the plains, especially around Sibi.

Flock of lambs and kids grazing.

Water resources are also something of a problem. In the hot season sheep need to be watered three times a day and goats at least once, while in winter sheep drink only once a day, and goats every other day. With few localized watering places, the areas for available pasture in critical seasons is limited, thus necessitating considerable local knowledge on the part of the shepherds.

The different species and age groups of domestic animals have different preferences and requirements in pastures and therefore must be herded separately. Women, children, and old men take the cattle and donkeys out to appropriate pastures in the morning and bring them back at night. Adult sheep and goats are herded separately, usually in the higher hill and mountain ranges, under the supervision of young men. Lambs and kids are kept together, usually closer to camp, in the charge of small children. Occasionally, sick animals are tied up at home, as are newborn lambs the first few days. The latter are also carried on migration by the children. Camels require separate herding.

For each herd of sheep or goats, the Marri deem it sufficient to keep from two to four stud males. There is no selection, but breeding is controlled to the extent that impregnation is prevented during two or three months in summer to avoid lambing during the winter, when the risk of loss is greatest. For goats, breeding is controlled by a device known as *tiddi*—a plaited dwarf-palm mat, about twelve inches square, tied under the male's belly and covering the genitals. This effectively prevents it from penetrating the female and makes it possible to keep all the goats in one joint herd. Rams, on the other hand, are separated from the main flock of female sheep and herded together with the lambs and kids during this period.

Shearing is generally done in spring and autumn, preceded by sheep-dipping. For shearing, the sheep is placed on a dwarf-palm mat, with bound feet, and then shorn, starting from the tail, working forward on the right side and then backward on the left. The bundle of wool from one sheep (*gorri*) is sprinkled with water and sheep dung to bind it together. If shearing is done by a person other than the owner, he receives 1 rupee for every 40 sheep, as well as a large bundle of wool (*harrol gorri:* "the bundle of the shears") for his labor and a meal of bread fried in butter.

Animals are private property, in the sense that they are frequently owned by one man (a few also by women) and carry his mark clipped in their ears, or they may be owned collectively by a small group of related men, who have fractional rights to the collective herd, and use a joint earmark. In either case, however, several elementary families living in separate tents usually subsist on the herd and are engaged in its care. The men in these subsistence units are usually related as sons to the owner of the flock or are brothers sharing an undivided patrimony. In either case, such an extended family group will normally provide a varied labor force of old people, young men, and children, suitable for the various shepherding roles. When it is necessary to supplement this force because of the composition of the family or the size of the herd, help is hired. The hired shepherd is then paid an annual wage of 40–100 rupees, food for himself but not for his family, one-eighth of the wool, one-sixth of the male lambs, and one-seventh of the female lambs of the herds. Animals may also be turned over to nomad shepherds on boarding or harboring contracts, by other nomads or by sedentary owners. The terms of such contracts depend on their duration. For a six-month contract owner and shepherd divide the newborn lambs in the ratio of three to one. For a full year the ratio of two to one for lambs and kids and equal division of the wool is common. In a four-year contract for goats the shepherd received one-fourth of the original herd and their female offspring at the end of the contract period, as well as half of all male kids and half the goat-hair produced each year. In all such harboring contracts it is understood that the shepherd gets all the milk.

All Marris have equal rights of access to pastures and water throughout the Marri tribal area. However, until the accession of the present Sardar Khair Bakhsh II, owners of herds of forty or more head had to pay a tax (*gahl*) of Rs. 4 to the sardar. Also, the external administration has imposed a government grazing tax (*tirni*). In areas outside their tribal lands, Marris pay the *gahl* tax to the tribal chiefs dominating the area. From being a variable offering of one or two animals, this tax has been fixed by a Marri-Luni agreement in the case of Luni Pathan lands as one lamb for each flock of sheep and one kid for each flock of goats. But constant frictions develop over the question, since the Marri try to avoid paying, while the different headmen and chiefs of Luni Pathan villages and sections each demand the tax in succession, and a new tax is demanded every time a tribal boundary is crossed, no matter how brief the visit may be.

Agriculture. In contrast to pasture areas, rights to agricultural land in the Marri area are vested in particular sections or even persons. Communal ownership within lineage segments, associated with periodic reallotment, is regarded as the traditional form, but some land has long been individually owned and other fields have recently been permanently subdivided. Communal land is held jointly in various localities by large groups on the second level of tribal segmentation (cf. Appendix I), such as Loharani and Powadhi. These lands are allotted to the constituent subsections, who may divide them among themselves and do farming on their own lands or give the land on tenancy contracts to others and divide the crop. Reallotments take place periodically, every ten, fourteen, or twenty years. The land is then divided by *mardansari* or *kermez* ("per male" and "straight as male urine," respectively), that is, every male person in the owning tribal section receives an equal share, whether he is born the day before the reallotment or dies the day after. But this equality is practiced only if the man is also of good blood on his mother's side; sons of a slave or low-caste mother will not receive a share.

Privately owned land is held by men and inherited in the male line; it is alienable, supposedly within the limits set by Islamic law. The right to hold individual title to land used to be a privilege associated with political office but is no longer so restricted.

Marris mainly cultivate cereals, of which wheat is the most important. Some of the settled communities base their agriculture in part on artificial irrigation from wells, springs, and *kermez*. In the Marri tribal area, however, only some 800 acres are supposed to be irrigated; the rest is dry land. Most fields depend on rainfall, but a special technique is utilized to assure sufficient moisture, somewhat simpler but essentially similar to that practiced by neighboring Pathan tribes. By this technique, the run-off following monsoon rainstorms is led, or permitted to flow naturally with the slope of the land, into the fields in the valley bottom. There it is retained by earthen embankments up to 6–8 feet high. The trapped water is then permitted to percolate into the ground, soaking the earth thoroughly. As soon as the surface water has disappeared, the fields are plowed and sowed broadcast on the artificially produced lake beds. The new wheat sprouts in October or November and is able to develop and ripen successfully without any further water, though the mild winter rains, if they occur, greatly enhance its growth. Manuring is unnecessary under this system, since the surface water washes considerable masses of silt, soil, and organic material into the cultivated areas. The crop ripens in April or May. Space for threshing is then prepared by sweeping, wetting, and stamping an area close to the field. Bullocks are used to trample the cut crop, and winnowing is done with a pronged winnowing fork.

Certain patterns of division of labor between the sexes emerge in agriculture: men do plowing and sowing, while men and women cooperate in threshing and winnowing. More important is the differentiation between owner and tenant, whereby much land is cultivated by persons other than the owner on a sharecropping basis. The contracts governing the division in shares vary considerably, depending on the fertility of the land, who owns seed and draft animals, what political conditions prevail, and whether the land is irrigated. Where the irrigation is supervised by persons other than the cultivator, they receive one-eleventh of the gross crop for their labor. If tenants provide seed, tools, and draft animals in dry-land farming, they generally receive half of the crop; in Luni territory they receive only six-thirteenths. When they provide only labor, they receive one-third or sometimes only one-fourth.

A field may thus be held on collective tenure by a dispersed group of owners, or the members of such a group may have changing fields temporarily allocated to them on rotation. Thus, the owners of land frequently reside at a great distance from their landed property. They are therefore rarely able to supervise their tenants effectively and frequently do not even bother to make the attempt. Joint owners will often sublet the undivided estate to a single tenant and merely send a representative either to collect the landlord's share of the crop or to sell it and return with the profits; even that is frequently not done. "This year and last year we didn't send anyone—we were busy with other work, and so on. It is a long journey." In such cases, the owners are resigned to taking an actual reduction in their profits, when they finally get around to collecting them.

"Part of it they eat, a little they give to us. Just as you'd give your servant Rs. 100 to buy things at the bazaar, and he'd buy some things and give you some money and take some for himself. And our shepherds—when they return and say a wolf has eaten a lamb, how are we to know they have not sold him and taken the money? All this is the same way. It's not in our hands—it's in the hands of strangers [gharib]. What we get depends on the honor [gind-i-iman] of the plowman or the shepherd."

Labor. Paid labor offers a third basis for subsistence. The preceding description has implied various opportunities for labor and tenancy contracts within Marri territory for people lacking the capital to be fully self-employed. But in the plains areas of Sindh there is also a seasonal labor market of great importance to many Marris. Numerous persons and camps travel to the plains to work in the fields during harvest time—in the case of the wheat harvest, in return for one-fortieth share of the crop. Small groups or families may also spend a considerable part of the winter in Sindh, where they work at the maintenance of the irrigation system and "clean the canals during the day and steal rice at night." Some also engage in haulage and trade.

Collecting. Finally, hunting and especially collecting contribute something to subsistence. Water and firewood are of course collected—by women, sometimes using the donkeys for transport. Dwarf palm is an important raw product, from which sandals, mats, tents, rope, and packsaddles are made; and the collection of high-quality dwarf-palm fronds is an important duty of the women. Honey and wild fruits, wild onions, and tender shoots and edible roots are also highly prized and sought after by mixed groups. Each of these resources has a variable distribution in time and space, only imperfectly known, and private knowledge of the terrain and their occurrences affects the movements of persons and camps. In the barren environment of the Marris, these additional sources of food are highly valued.

"Mohammed Sharif and Bibi were living with a rich man, Bibi working for him while the Prophet went around doing his prophet work. When Bibi finished baking the bread for the rich man, she washed the dough off her hands and made it into bread for the children, and in that way they lived. But one day the rich man came as she was washing her hands and scolded her, saying she left a lot of the dough on her hands on purpose, just for her children, and forbade her to do that in the future. So Bibi got mad and shook the water off her hands on to the ground, making a prayer that God would give enough food so that her children could pass their days and sleep their nights. And where the drops from her left hand fell grew onions, and from her right hand grew dwarf palm and the edible wild cactus. So the children ate the tender dwarf palm stalks in the spring, the tender palm-fruit seeds in the rainy season, and the ripe fruits in the autumn. They ate the cactus raw as they found it on the hillside in the autumn, and boiled it in the winter. And at all seasons they had onions."

The economic units that engage in such pursuits are, as noted, generally larger than the elementary family and are thus composed of the residents of several tents or rooms in a compound. The consumption rate of the joint family forming such a household unit will of course depend on the size of the group and on its wealth. A joint family of eleven persons, which was regarded as average in its standard of living, consumed Rs. 100 worth of wheat per month, as well as considerable quantities of meat. It is important to note with respect to the consumption of households that, no matter which combination of subsistence activities a family pursues, its actual diet will tend to be the same; wheat and meat are the staples of all. The households that do not themselves produce the traditional balance of products will obtain what they need through exchange. In addition, a variety of goods is required that Marris are not themselves able to produce and that they are forced to obtain through trade, particularly cloth, tea, sugar, matches, and various luxury items.

Most of this trade, as well as much of the internal circulation of wheat, is in the hands of a small caste of Hindu merchants. These Hindus are Hindko-speaking and regard Kalat as their homeland, where they generally keep their families and go for some months every year to visit and to obtain supplies. While in the Marri area, they must be under the protection of a local Marri chief or the sardar himself. In return for this protection, and as a tax on their trade, they pay their patron Rs. 1/8/- for every camel load they bring into the area and one-tenth of the gross grain crop they obtain for their goods. Because of the relative insecurity of the area and the bulkiness of the goods that are handled, most such trade takes place in a shop or trading post close to the residence of the chief.

Marri subsistence thus revolves around pasturage, cultivation, and cash labor in Sindh and requires intermittent contact by every household with a trading post. In various combinations, these factors determine the form of residence patterns and migratory movements. A simple three-fold division is often used to classify the population according to residence type: the Marri generally distinguish between villager and tent-dweller, subdividing the latter into *darshin*—who are structurally connected with a village and move locally within the circumference of its district—and *powindah*—who move in relation to water and seasonal pastures and whose camps are units unto themselves.

Perhaps a more useful picture emerges if one constructs a threefold typology of community types. (1) In the Marri area there are a few large compact villages with substantial sedentary populations. Each such village is also the center for the surrounding populations of nomads (*darshin*). (2) In most areas, however, the compact village is lacking, and only its nucleus is found: a small cluster of mud houses containing the residence of a local chief or notable and his collaterals who are landowners, a Hindu's shop and house, and perhaps the home of a mullah or a craftsman. In the close neighborhood one also finds the scattered tents of tenants cultivating the fields of the landowners, and in the surrounding districts again are found the attached population of *darshin* nomads. (3) Finally, there are the small camps of *powindahs*, relatively free-moving nomads. The latter communities are of course, with respect to size, of quite a different order from the two former but may nonetheless form communities as autonomous as do types 1 and 2. In composition and economy, however, they are not unlike the *darshin* segments of the larger communities and, through a restriction of the migratory circuit and the development of economic and political bonds with one village, may readily become *darshin*—just as the *darshin* may become *powindah* through the reverse process. I shall now describe each of these community types consecutively, in some greater detail.

1. Of the large villages, a special case is Kahan, since it is the traditional center of the whole Marri tribe and contains the fortress that used to be the residence of the sardar. Until recently, Kahan contained about 400 occupied houses, although many of the houses belonged to section chiefs and were inhabited by them only irregularly. Most of the permanent population was *Mareta* ("slave") or other non-Marri serfs. Today, as a result of the sardar's change of residence to Quetta, the government's decision to locate its administrative center 50 miles north in Kohlu, and a series of ruinous droughts, Kahan has been depopulated and retains scarcely twenty resident households.

The other large old villages, however, continue to thrive and grow and range in size from about 200 to 1,000 inhabitants. They are mostly located in the north (the Kohlu Valley) and along the western borders of the Marri area, and all seem to have been originally Pathan villages that were conquered but not, as were many others, demolished. Their Marri population tends to be mixed, though dominance is in the hands of one of the resident tribal sections; in addition they may contain a remnant of the old Pathan population and persons of other castes (Hindu, Lori, etc.).

Thus, for example, the village of Badra was conquered by the Marri from the Baruzai Pathans. According to tradition, the village was held by Mohammed Gharib Khan Baruzai on a grant from the amir of Afghanistan.

"The Marris were defeated by a local tribe called the Hasani [cf. p. 4] and some were driven toward Sindh. With the help of the khan of Kalat the Marris defeated the Hasanis later and regained Kahan. Some of the Marris who had gone to Sindh remained there, some returned to Marri area, but rather than remaining in Kahan came and captured Badra from Pathans. These people who had lived for a time in Sindh are called Sindhis."

"Badra area was held by 11 [Barozai] men. They could not control the area because they were new there and could not get the support of other Pathan tribes. The present Marri *Maretas* are descendants of slaves of the Barozai."

Badra now has a population of about 300 persons, plus 800–900 nomads in the neighboring hills. It is dominated by two families of the Sindhi section of the Langhanis (see Appendix I) and is mainly inhabited by that section. The 50–60 Pathans in the village are of Musa Khel, Khajak, and Abdullah Khel descent, the last being the former subjects of the Baruzai. In addition, there are four shop-keepers, one Lori (low-caste) household, a beggar "called Haji because he has a long beard [the mark of having made the pilgrimage to Mecca]. He is a greedy fellow. He has placed himself under our protection." A school was built in 1949, and there is a Panjabi schoolteacher. The village has a mullah, and there is also, rather exceptional for Marris, a small colony of Sayyids (descendants of the

Prophet). "We have given the Sayyids some sections of land. They learn to read and write from the mullahs in the mosque" and are used to draw up documents and keep accounts. An essentially similar picture holds true for the villages of the Kohlu valley, where, however, Sayyids are lacking, and the local Pathans belong to other tribes.

The economy of the village population depends heavily on agriculture, but large herds are also kept, under the supervision of one or several communal shepherds. The surrounding *darshin* are mostly mixed herders and cultivators, as owners or tenants; those entirely without capital may also be full-time agricultural laborers or full-time shepherds for the village flocks.

2. Only a small fraction of the Marri tribe is organized in and around large village settlements; the predominant pattern is the second type of community based on only a small sedentary nucleus. This nucleus is established at the initiative of a chief or notable and has less permanence than the large villages—it may be abandoned as his fortunes decline or his interests shift to a different area, where a new settlement nucleus is equally readily constructed. These village nuclei generally carry the name or title of the original founder or the present leader, with the ambitious suffix -*shahr*, meaning "city." They automatically become the site of the shop of the Hindu trading in the area, any settled craftsmen practicing in the district, etc. With the leader are also usually found at least some of his close collaterals, all together making up a population of from four to ten elementary families or up to forty persons.

Closely tied to this settlement are usually at least an equal number of people, either as tenants or serfs on the lands of the leader and his collaterals or as hired shepherds for their flocks. These persons are functionally equivalent to village residents in the larger villages, but in the village nucleus communities they live in palm-mat tents or brush shelters in the neighborhood, scattered over an area of some square miles. Unless they are tied to their employers as serfs or slaves, these people are somewhat more mobile than their village counterparts, perhaps mainly because of the lack of investment in a permanent residence and the equipment that goes with it. Though destitute and economically dependent on their employers, they thus tend to form a rather free-floating population of migratory labor; if they own but a single donkey, they can escape on labor migrations to Sindh, and, in any case, they may change their place of employment. Of the persons in this category with whom the Pehrsons worked in 1955, many were widely scattered in distant places by 1960, when I attempted to trace them.

The remaining and far largest fraction of the population that has the village nucleus as its center is made up of tent-dwelling nomads—who own flocks but also engage heavily in agriculture. The total community constituted in this way, including both its nucleus and periphery, may range in population from 200 to 1,000 individuals.

The camps of this nomadic section are very small, comprising from one to five

Village nucleus: residence of a section chief, shopkeeper, etc.

tents only; their migratory circuit is restricted because of their vested interest in land and crops and their dependence on the village nucleus for trade and political support. "I have about 30 animals. I live here and there and there and there [pointing in a circling movement around the horizon]. Ten-fifteen-twenty days in one place and then a new place. When coming to a new place the heart becomes new."

3. A difference in the amount of capital they own is the main factor that under-lies the difference in migratory pattern and community identity between the *darshin* of the village nucleus communities and the *powindah* nomads. Once the herd reaches about one hundred animals, its value is so great that other consid-erations become secondary compared with the welfare of the herd, and unless very favorably situated the camp then breaks loose from its village nucleus, mi-grating widely in search of pasture and water. Even when such herd-owners also own considerable land, its care becomes a matter of secondary importance. "The big animal owners who move to Chamalang buy their wheat, since their own lands are back in Kahan, Kohlu, and other parts of Marristan." "The big herd owners (*bhaggia*) have no land. They run away." The actual balance that is established between herding and agriculture depends, however, on convenience and opportunities and may change from one year to the next.

"We move because of our animals, whose wool and lambs we sell. We sell no wheat but eat it all ourselves. The reason we do this plowing is that thanks be to Allah we are many brothers and have surplus men from herding needs. [In 1952] we moved to the Quet-Mondai area, since the Luni territory was closed to us because of the Marri-Luni war. There we did no agricultural work."

The leader of the same camp, when permission to plow in the area was refused by the Luni sardar in 1955, commented:

"That's all right, we are primarily animal owners and if we can graze here that is enough for us. We can always do plowing in adjacent non-Luni areas, but we really don't have to do it."

The factors that enter into the decisions regarding allocation of labor and migratory route and schedule are thus very complex, and, since they are sensitive to irregularities in precipitation, labor market, and political relations, each camp is faced with the problem of imperfect information. The second- and third-hand news collected through the institution of *hal* (a formalized grapevine system, cf. pp. 73, 75), is rarely sufficiently reliable; as a result, camp members are sent out to scout for good areas in the general neighborhood and even to visit distant areas to collect information on pastures, political climate, density of nomadic camps, and opportunities for plowing contracts. On the basis of such information, the timing and direction of migrations are determined, and, though for each camp the alternatives are in fact limited by such relatively constant considerations as previous experience and habit, the size of herds, the labor capacity of the household, etc., there is much variation in the movements of a camp from one year to the next. Each of the different alternatives has its advantages and disadvantages. "I don't like to do this because with this kind of schedule there is plenty of war, theft, and trouble. . . ."

For Marri nomads as a whole, a bewildering variety of movements results, with no clear predominant patterns—caravans on migration regularly intersect or meet, some going up when others go down. A few standard trends, however, may be observed. In the hot season of summer there is a general movement toward the higher ranges, which expresses itself in a general shifting northward, where the average altitude rises. This brings large Marri populations out of the Marri tribal area and into Pathan country around Sanjawi, Loralai, and Mekhtar, while camps from lower and southern areas congregate in the Kohlu valley and adjoining districts. If the monsoons fail, however, those who remain in the southern areas around Kahan may be driven in the opposite direction, southward into the lowlands of Sindh, where their fewer, more heat-resistant animals can survive, though hardly prosper, by grazing along irrigated fields or in waterlogged areas.

In the autumn, Afghan *powindah* tribes descend on the northern areas of Duki and Loralai, where they spend the winter. Since there is traditional enmity between them and the Marris and since Marri sheep are considerably less tolerant of cold, the Marris in the north then tend to fall back into the Marri area or to the lowest fringes of Duki Tahsil or eastward to the lower Khetran lands of Barkhan and Vitakri. The camps that winter in the relatively higher areas often construct more permanent winter huts (*juggi*) of trees and branches covered with palm-leaf mats while occupied, as well as thorn and branch shelters for the protection of the herds. Some even build mud huts for themselves. These winter-camp structures are inherited patrilineally and tend to lead to a regularizing of the owners' migratory route.

The far-ranging nomads must also have social contact with sedentary society and access to trading posts—that is, they must find an institutional alternative to the relationship with the village nucleus on which the locally migrating nomads depend. This alternative takes the form of an institutionalized, favored village-friend relationship (to a partner called *bradir*), which is common among all Marri nomads but of particular importance to those who travel widely. The *bradir* should be an unrelated man and may even be from another tribe—although Hindu traders are ineligible, no matter how stable their connection with any particular Marri may be. As the latter fact implies, not all commercial transactions take place within the framework of institutionalized friendship; nor is the relationship solely or necessarily a trading relationship. It is always a reciprocal host-guest relationship and is an important source of information about camp movement and economic opportunities in strange areas. Through a network of such relationships a social universe of some degree of security and intimacy is created, within which persons may with greater confidence cross territorial and political dividing lines and the gulf between nomad and villager. The relationship is essentially a dyadic one between the two friends but tends to produce some acquaintance with other members of the partner's community. It also tends to persist and be passed on from father to son, but lapses unless it is periodically activated.

"In Kohlu I now have no *bradir*. They have all died and I have been away so long that no one knows me. When I am there my bread is given by [my section chief]. The hill Marris around Kohlu have their *bradir* among the villages there. My brothers and I decided to come to this area because it had good grass and water and because there was possibility for plowing work. With time I have made many *bradir* both with the village Pathans and with the Afghan *powindahs*. It is natural that my son should be the *bradir* of my *bradir*'s sons, since they know that he is my son and since I have taken him with me to the villages. I have made my *bradirs* among honorable men. N. N.—a thief—makes his with thieves."

This mutual *bradir* relationship must be distinguished from the more strictly political and administrative relationships of patronage and support between section chiefs and commoners, however, which are defined by descent and section membership and persist regardless of physical distance. The structure of which they form a part will be the subject of the next chapter.

III

FORMAL TRIBAL SYSTEM OF THE MARRI

THE FORMAL organizational charter of the Marri tribe consists of a merging series of sections with a congruent series of offices, occupied by a hierarchy of leaders of sections. Recruitment to sections tends to follow from patrilineal descent, but the crucial principle is that of political contract between leader and follower, and such contracts may be entered without reference to descent position. Authority in the system is conceived as flowing from the central chief, and the system is maintained by a rigid restriction and canalization of the flow of communications.

The Marri tribe constitutes a clearly delimited political unit; it also is conceived of by its members and their neighbors as an ethnic subcategory of the Baluch and as a population interrelated by kinship and descent (i.e., a *kaum*). Marris draw in the sand the position of their tribe vis-à-vis other Baluch tribes, as shown in Figure 1. Different Pathan tribes are conceptualized as clustering in a similar way in a Pathan grouping. Yet the Marris also regard territorial contiguity as important, in contradiction to the categorical boundaries that such an ethnic taxonomy creates. Thus Marris who were cospectators with the Pehrsons to a Pathan dance in a Marri-dominated village commented: "If these Pathans lived in a different area far away in Baluchistan somewhere, then their dance would be different. These Pathans live in Badra, so their dance is the same as the Marris'. . . . However far away the lands are, then the customs are that far apart."

Within the tribe, a Marri will identify himself as a member of a particular section and subsection. When strangers meet, they identify each other's position through a process of specifying such sections and subsections down to the level that has relevance in terms of the questioner's knowledge: Who are you? Marri. What Marri? Ghazeni (this level may be skipped). What Ghazeni? Longhani. What Longhani? Muliani. And frequently: What is your name? Bangul. With increasing specificity the eponymal suffixes in such series generally shift from *-eni* or *-ani* to *-zai*. Asked to diagram these differentiations, Marris will again represent the sections on each level, exemplified by the main three sections of the tribe (Fig. 2). A copy of the Kohlu Tahsil record showing Marri sections and subsections, and their leaders, as of January 1, 1940, is given in Appendix I.

On the higher levels of segmentation, sections and subsections are known as *tākār;* on lower levels, *khanadan* and *khel* may be used, while the minimal lineage is properly known as *waris.* Alternatively, *firqa* may be used apparently synonymously with *tākār,* while the main three sections of the tribe are often referred to as *saiyāk* ("thirds"). Subsections, to emphasize their position vis-à-vis the more inclusive section, are also called *shakh* ("horn" or "prong").

The main trisectioning of the tribe is traditionally established but is being challenged on two points. The position of Shiranis as a segment of the Loharani is a problem. Other groups regard them as members of a comprehensive group, Loharani, but the Shirani claim to be an independent major section. Likewise, the Powadhi no longer accept their traditional structural position as one of the twelve sections of the Bijaranis but speak of themselves in opposition to Bijaranis as sections of coordinate level. These disagreements relate to growth and segmentation as historical processes, to be discussed later; but they also relate to the question of what precisely are the formal criteria of grouping in the tribal system.

FIGURE 1   FIGURE 2

To this question there is no clear and unequivocal answer in Marri culture. Tribal sections are conceived as groups simultaneously recruited by patrilineal descent, sharing rights in an estate in the form of agriculture land and acknowledging the authority of a leader. There is no canonical justification for the necessity of agreement between these apparently separate criteria.

In everyday contexts the first of these criteria is generally regarded as basic and is referred to, for example, in the form of proverbs: "My duty is Bijarani, just as my bones are Bijarani." Local groups are based on patriliny and patrilocality, reckoning of kinship has its clear agnatic bias, rights to private property are transmitted in agnatic line or held jointly by agnatic groups, etc. The whole tribal structure can thus be thought of as an enormous agnatic lineage. Yet the genealogical charter for such a lineage structure is entirely lacking—the structure is one of named groups and subgroups, not of ancestors, and the pedigrees of tribesmen can rarely be traced more than three or four generations. Also, historical traditions of accretion and confederational growth of sections are common; and, when challenged, few informants will insist on the descent unity of any section.

Informants explaining the accretional origin of their section may refer to other conditions in former times: "In those days there was war and anarchy. Nobody asked who is your father, brother. You joined in the fighting force, moved and conquered and moved again. Later only did it become fixed and settled like now."

The full member of a tribal section is given a share (*wānd*) in that section's landed estate. Such shares are usually granted to persons on the basis of their agnatic status, as the patrilineal descendants, with two important restrictions: only males receive a share and are regarded as full members; furthermore, males of impeccable patrilineal descent, but from a mother of low caste, may be considered tainted by their mother's low status and denied a share in the section's estate.

The periodic (often every ten or every fourteen years) reallotments of tribal lands are the occasions for the review of sectional membership through the distribution of shares. Down to a certain point, the division of the joint estate follows the schema of segmentation into subgroups; below that point, the subgroups are treated as unsegmented corporations and full members are given equal shares regardless of age, household organization, and genealogical interconnections. Thus, for example, the Nozbandagani section of the Ghazeni divide their joint estate between the section's effective subdivisions in the proportions Rhazenzai 4 : Jafozai 4 : Baikanzai 2 : Waderazai 2 : Pahnkanzai 2 : Moralzai 1 : Ghevezai 1. This agrees with the charter of segmentation of the group, as shown in Figure 3. Within each of these effective subdivisions, all members share equally.

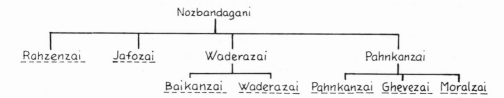

Nozbandagani

Rahzenzai   Jafozai   Waderazai   Pahnkanzai

Baikanzai Waderazai   Pahnkanzai Ghevezai Moralzai

FIGURE 3

Though the fact of receiving a share may be seen as a crucial confirmation of full membership in a tribal section, it cannot serve for the group itself as the criterion of inclusion or exclusion but must in turn be based on one or several such criteria. Furthermore, the currency of traditions of confederation and accretion in sections indicates that patrilineal descent is not the only criterion. Other possible criteria of membership are revealed in the contract or fiction that is established when a stranger without an initial agnatic position is assimilated to the section.

"If I were to come as a refugee to Badra I would ask permission to be a political client [*hamsayah*] of Haji Karim Dad. If he said "No" then I would go to the Langhani leader [*Wadera*], who would give me permission. We intermarry [i.e., with commoners of the section], and my children become N. N.-zai Langhani. One does not ask permission of the small men."

In former times, joining a group in war was another standard way of becoming incorporated into it as a member. Particularly where conquest of land resulted, such incorporation would be stable; but participation in the defense of a territory, and even mere participation in looting, seems regularly to have resulted in incorporation in the group under whose leader one fought. Marris agree that this was a common occurrence and thus recognize the origins of the personnel of any one section to have been diverse. The Marri tribe and its sections must·thus be understood as a structure of *groups and leaders,* and the crucial feature of membership in a group is the relationship of subordination to its leader. Such a relationship may spring either from birth into an agnatic household already so placed or from a contract of submission entered into by an adult man with a leader.

Bearing in mind the structure of sections and subsections, we must therefore investigate the consonant hierarchy of leaders and political offices. As a first approximation, one can see a clear hierarchy of offices from the sardar, the chief of the tribe, through, in part, double echelons of leaders called either wadera or mukadam, down to the leaders of minimal lineages, who are called mutabar (a generic word for leader but used particularly with reference to these rather modest positions of leadership), and, finally, in every camp or settlement, a halk-waja, or camp leader.

The sardar is the central and unifying leader, who by his existence creates the Marri tribe and who for formal purposes is regarded as the fount of all legitimate power in the tribe. The common attitude of respect for the sardar, often approaching awe and ascribing magical and superhuman qualities to the person of the sardar, is very striking and also encompasses attitudes which elsewhere in the Middle East are reserved for saints and other holy men. Succession to sardarship is patrilineal, to eldest sane son by a mother of clean caste.

The present ruling dynasty is the Bahawalan section of the Ghazeni. Present tradition, and traditions recorded about 1880 (Duke 1883), agree on the details of genealogy and succession back to the eponymous ancestor Bahawalan, which places him at seven generations' depth from the present Marri Sardar Khair Bakhsh II. The traditional residence of the sardar is Kahan, and, though the present chief has resided permanently in Quetta for some years, Kahan has continued to serve as the tribal center until very recently, and the sardar has been expected to preside there for brief periods in his crumbling fortress. Now, Kahan has been superseded in importance by Kohlu, the seat of the representatives of Pakistani central authorities.

The sardar's exalted position of authority in the tribal structure is supported by several important sources of power, most notably a considerable wealth, various privileged sources of income, and the power, within limits, to withhold the confirmation of succession to lower positions and to create new ones.

The nucleus of the sardar's wealth is constituted by an entailed estate called *pag* (literally, "turban"; idiomatically, "crown") property. Whereas all other wealth is inherited equally by all the sardar's sons, this estate passes intact to his successor and includes lands and houses around Kahan and elsewhere in the Marri area. In former times, when Marri conquered new lands in warfare the sardar would receive one-fifth (*panjah*) of such land and other loot as his share.

Other privileged sources of income are various. The traditional right to collect an annual tax of one sheep in every twenty-five was exercised by previous sardars but has been renounced by Khair Bakhsh II. The sardar also has the right to levy special taxes as contributions toward the bride-prices of his marriages. He receives half of all fines collected by tribal courts in criminal cases. As part of the settlement after a conflict between the Marri and the British, he was given taxation rights in the areas of Quet-Mondai and Badra, formerly not parts of Marri Tribal Area. The British also encouraged him to institute a small levies group directly under his control, based on a subsidy of Rs. 3,000. Before that the sardar had no regular force at his command other than his private servants and slaves, but depended on his authority to command services and obedience from any and every Marri. The total annual income of the Marri sardar is estimated by knowledgable informants at about Rs. 50,000.[1]

Finally, the sardar has power over subordinate leaders through his role in confirming their succession and his authority to nominate and call on persons to participate in the tribal court councils in which political decisions are made. Conversely, however, this group of leaders plays an essential role in confirming the sardar's succession.

This confirmation becomes important because the rules of succession are in practice neither as clear nor as absolute as they might seem, and rivalries have arisen in every recent case of succession, sometimes leading to fratricide, external interference in the form of the offer of bribes, and internal factionalism. An important factor that leaves room for manipulation is the purity of blood of the pretenders' mothers—the sardar has generally been surrounded by a harem of wives and has had issue by slaves, low-caste women, commoners, women of noble line, and daughters of neighboring sardars, khans, and nawabs. The formal choice of successor is thus made, usually among several candidates with competing claims, by the tribal council in the form of a ceremonial investiture, which takes place under the leadership of a mullah. The crowning ceremony is the tying of the new sardar's turban by the assembled section leaders, each winding one loop of the immensely long turban around the sardar's head.

The wadera is to his section what the sardar is to the tribe as a whole. Waderaship is vested in noble lines and passes to lineal descendants, confirmed by a turban-tying ceremony in which the sardar winds the first loop. Like the sardar,

---

1. In contrast, that of the Bugti sardar, who is the head of the neighboring Baluch tribe, with an analogous, though more effectively autocratic, structure, was estimated at about Rs. 300,000, before the recent land reforms, which have now reduced his extratribal estates.

a wadera is given an entailed estate and has the right to one-fifth share of what
his section conquers in battle, as well as the right to irregular tax (*loht*) for special purposes, such as paying bride-prices. A special position is that of the rahzen,
a hereditary title in the Nozbandagani section, which also has its wadera. The
rahzen is described as the second-in-command of the Marri tribe: "There is only
one rahzen in our tribe. He is the most brave man of all the Marris." The term
also means "leader" and "highwayman"; his special role in warfare is variously
described as leading the charge or as following the troops into battle, cutting
down those who turn to flee from the enemy.

Mukadams, on the other hand, do not hold strictly hereditary titles. Though
there is a distinct tendency for sons to succeed their fathers as mukadams, the
difference can be seen in the rules regarding regenthood. When the son of a
sardar, rahzen, or wadera is under-age at the death of his father, he is nonetheless
confirmed in his succession, but a senior collateral agnate is then appointed as
regent until the boy comes of age, as was Doda Khan, the deceased sardar's
brother, when Khair Bakhsh II succeeded at the age of seven. Likewise with
waderas and rahzen:

"When Khair Mohammed Rahzen died, his brother Sher Mohammed became regent.
When Sher Mohammed died, his son Azad Khan [who was his second son, but the
eldest 'was weak'] claimed to be rahzen. But Khair Mohammed's son Mohammed
Rahzen felt the title was his and contended with Azad Khan and took the case to the
sardar and the tribal council in Kahan. The council decided in Mohammed Rahzen's
favor, and the sardar bound the turban on his head."

Mukadams, on the other hand, are replaced by the agnate best qualified by wealth
and influence to fill the position, so the title frequently passes to a collateral line.
Also, while the number of *pag* waderas is fixed, the sardar is free to create new
mukadams, and there is historical evidence that the whole category "mukadam"
is a relatively recent innovation, by which the sardar was encouraged, if not actu-
ally instigated, by the British to contain the influence of the waderas.

The power of the rahzen, waderas and mukadams springs ultimately, like that
of the sardar, from wealth, income, and a few special privileges. Only such men
were traditionally allowed to own private land, all other land being subject to
periodic redistribution within sections. Augmented by irregular taxing, fines, etc.,
the income of such leaders may reach about 20,000 rupees per annum, though
most fall much lower.

Almost all these leaders among the Marri are now settled; they usually preside
over a small cluster of houses of the village nucleus type,(cf. p. 134), exercising economic control over laborers and tenants and gaining influence over the
nomads of the surrounding district not only by their formal office but also by
controlling their trade relations through the resident Hindu merchant, whom they
also tax. The most important source of power for this group of leaders, however,

is their membership in the tribal council. This council (*jirga*), as it has been developed among the Marri, is the central institution on which the whole tribal structure rests. In it the hierarchy of tribal leaders, the organs of external administration, and the framework of sections meet and articulate in a manner that is decisive to the function of each.

The nature of the Marri tribal council cannot be understood without reference to administrative organs outside the tribe. Whatever it may have been previously, Sandeman's "Forward Policy" of indirect rule (Bruce 1900) and the later Frontier Crimes regulation have made it into, among other things, a court of law that functions as an organ of the external administration.

The formal system for tribal administration was developed by the British in India and has largely been retained unchanged by the Pakistanis. As far as it has direct reference to the Marris, its formal schema is as follows:

> Assistant governor general
> Political agent (P.A.), Sibi
>   District intertribal councils
> Assistant political agent (A.P.A.)
> Extra assistant commissioner (E.A.C.), Marri/Bugti
>   Marri tribal council
> Tahsildar, Kohlu

In this system, tribal councils are used for the settlement of disputes of all sorts. When the parties belong to the same tribe, authority lies with the tribal council; when the parties belong to different tribes, the case is brought before an intertribal council of the two groups concerned. Evidence is taken by the council, and cases are judged by tribal custom law (*riwaj*). In cases in which imprisonment is considered necessary, the extent of the punishment is determined by the E.A.C. or the P.A., and the culprit is passed on to the government jail. Cases before the Marri tribal council are concerned about 50 per cent with theft of livestock and other movable property, 25 per cent with adultery, 5 per cent with blood revenge and compensation, 10 per cent with land disputes, and 10 per cent with miscellaneous offenses (beatings, quarrels, etc.).

Among the Marri it is also recognized that the tribal council can make new law and can change traditional custom law by council decision. The Marri tribal council is thus a very powerful body, which legislates, adjudicates, and, within limits set by the E.A.C., mobilizes the external force of government police and levies to effectuate its decisions.

The tribal council used to be called and presided over by the sardar. Today, this authority has been usurped by the external administration, and the council is convened by the P.A. and/or the E.A.C., though these officials do not themselves sit in on the council discussions. Council meetings are held at various places in Marri territory in a more or less regular yearly cycle, and joint meetings with neighboring tribes are held as intertribal councils on or near the boundaries. These larger intertribal councils are particularly exciting and festive occasions. Not only council members and litigants but also a great number of spectators congregate, temporary bazaars of tents and brush-hut shops spring up, and minstrels and beggars mix with throngs of people and riders. The proceedings themselves take place in the open and are very noisy and confused. Several scribes take down the evidence and the decisions—though formerly all was done orally—and around them are grouped the council members, or such of them as are present at the moment, seated on rugs. Sitting, squatting, and standing in concentric circles around them are litigants waiting for their cases to come up, witnesses to be called, and spectators. Occasionally a path is cleared for a woman, who is led in by her Fa, Hu, or Br to give evidence or plead her case in a whisper to one of the council members, while keeping her face and body hidden in her sari. Several cases are usually discussed simultaneously. Factional allies whisper to each other about strategy or depart from the circle to consult with each other. Occasionally an important man comes in and is formally greeted by the persons with whom he sits down. Payments, fines, and loans are transacted in public view so that the council can serve as witness to their completion. Amid all this movement, noise, and activity, decisions are arrived at without a formal vote and passed on to the government official, who is excluded from being present but who may in practice be consulted by messengers or the members themselves and who also sometimes chooses to return a case to the council for further discussion.

This is a formidable and frightening show for the non-member, who is at liberty to plead his case and try to catch the members' attention when called on but who must be quiet when ordered to be so and can take no part in whatever debate may develop around his case. For this reason, and because members mutually support each other's positions by insisting on the procedure, no commoner dares submit a case unless he has consulted a leader of his own section and been encouraged by a promise that he will personally intervene (*kuhla deyāgh*) on his client's behalf with prominent leaders.

This puts a new perspective on the power and influence of council members. Not only do they collectively wield great powers; each of them also controls, or serves as a channel for, communications between commoners of a particular section or subsection and the council as an adjudicating institution. Today, it would seem that wealth and income and other privileges mainly serve as the waderas' and mukadams' platform for competitive climbing and faction-formation, while their political power over inferiors, and thus the ultimate power associated with their rank, springs from their seats in the tribal council.

There are, however, two factors that might tend to contain this power. One is the fact of multiple representation of sections, the other the external administration's authority, acting in the name of the sardar, to appoint and remove members of the council.

The chart in Appendix I shows the sections and subsections and their leaders at a certain point of time. A closer inspection reveals numerous inconsistencies between the hierarchy of sections and the number and echelons of leaders. Several groups are listed with two or more leaders, some leaders are listed on one level of segmentation only, and others are listed as leaders both of a section and of one of its component subsections. These inconsistencies are empirically correct, both for the period of Pehrson's visit in 1955 and for my own visit in 1960. The native ideal, on the other hand, seems to be that of perfect fit and strict delineation of echelons of leaders, as in a military hierarchy. Deviations from this ideal they explain historically, either as a result of policy from above, encouraging rivalry by duplicating leaders, or as a result of the usurpation of lower-echelon positions by higher-echelon leaders.

The first of these processes has already been suggested in connection with the introduction of mukadam rank. The second seems to take place when a section or subsection loses its leader and his agnatic line, either because blood feuds exterminate the family or because they lose all influence because of incompetence. This creates a vacuum that tends to be filled from *above*, by superior echelon leaders who wish to cement their control over their section or seek strength against coordinate and rival leaders of the section.

Regardless of how this situation has come about, the presence of duplicate and of ranked leaders might offer certain strategic advantages to commoners. But these advantages are made negligible by the leaders' counterstrategy: where duplicate leaders are found, they impose de facto personal patronage claims each to their clearly identified group of clients, so the only manipulatory move left to the commoners is an explicit contractual breach and change of allegiance. Analogously, lower-echelon leaders, to retain any position of importance, realize that they must impose themselves as an obligatory channel of all vertical communications between commoners of their subsection and the leader of their section.

Nonetheless, fissive opposition groups may and at times do form with any leader's following, and this opposition has clearly been common also in past times. Formerly, such groups would break away and join other sections or tribes or perhaps form new sections of their own. Today, it appears that such movements are anticipated and utilized by the sardar and the administration for the appointment of duplicate leaders in an effort to control the tribe more effectively from the center.

The actual balance of power between the center and the lower levels of tribal organization is far from clear and turns on the extent of the center's freedom to appoint council members. Until now, the administration has been very careful and restrained in its exercise of such freedom, for reasons that are obvious. With the present system, peace is maintained in a large and very difficult area with relatively low expenditure and little use of force. A prerequisite is that the members of the council should command respect among the tribesmen. Thus, only persons with undoubted influence are useful members of the council, therefore hereditary leaders who are unable to assert their authority lose their place on the administration's list of council members. For example, one young wadera in my presence approached the E.A.C. and complained that no one listened to him, since he was given no authority from above. He was told that it was his own fault—that he should assert himself and exercise leadership, then people would respect him and the administration would recognize him. Among the politically sophisticated, indeed, the term *"pag-waja"* ("leader by the turban"), or person whose rank springs from pure descent, has the connotation of formal but ineffectual rank—the dynamic leaders tend to be those who have risen from less noble lines and who have imposed themselves on people and the administration and *won* mukadam rank.

Minor tribal leaders.

Yet, just as commoners are forced into a client relationship and made to act through the vertical channels of petition and pleading through their leaders, so the leaders themselves also see the organization in such lineal and hierarchical terms. They are awed by the leader in the center, by the sardar and the administrative officials, and they see their own position of influence as derived from their contact with this center. Thus the hierarchy is considered to depend on a flow of power from the center downward through the echelons of leaders: "I touch the political agent's boots, and get a thousand to touch mine."

The way in which the tribal council works is thus affected. There is little overt rallying of factions in debates, and no fusion of the leaders, for example, of one trisection of the tribe in opposition to those of another trisection. Instead, efforts are directed at winning the support of the most influential leaders or the sardar or the member who is rumored for the moment to serve as the E.A.C.'s mouth-piece. This is in clear contrast to the fusion-fission picture which the commoners have and follow in their loyalties to, and mobilization of, groups:

"I fight with my [agnatic] cousin but when another Muliani comes to fight me or him, then we are one. When a Londawani comes to fight a Muliani, then we are one. When a Mazarani comes to fight a Langhani, then we are one. In a war with the Bijaranis then all Ghazeni: Tingiani, Mazarani, Langhani, all—become one. In a war with Pathans all Marris are one."

The failure of leaders to exhibit similar sectional loyalties is recognized by the commoners; it causes regret but not surprise, since it fits well with the Marri picture of man as a self-seeking, opportunistic, and morally bad creature. On the other hand, the more unscrupulous leaders turn this commoners' attitude and suspicion to their own advantage, playing on the complexities of council politics to explain why their own supposed efforts in defense of their clients are not more clearly apparent from council procedures and how they failed because of bribery and other underhanded deals between council members, not disclosed in the debate. Indeed, several such leaders are widely accused of greatly increasing their income by soliciting money from their clients, to be used as bribes in support of their cases, and then pocketing the bribes, explaining the possible failure of the cases as the results of even larger bribes to council members from the other party (while attributing possible successes to the efficacy of bribes never given).

I would even suggest that this expectation of rapaciousness among leaders is an integral and necessary aspect of the Marri political structure. Its immediate effects are widespread and profound hesitation on the part of commoners to come into close and direct contact with their section leaders or to request their intervention or support. Even more, it leads to fear and avoidance of the leaders of other sections, lest, in addition to being fleeced also by them, one may call down the wrath and revenge of one's own patron upon one's self. Communications to men of rank are therefore few and preferably through men of intermediate rank; they are, further, often initiated by leaders who can cut them off at their pleasure. Thus great differences in rank can be maintained, and the intricacies of council politics become accepted as incomprehensible to the commoner, who therefore must continue in dependence on men of rank, since they alone understand the council's workings. As will be shown in later chapters, the isolation and mutual suspicion that obtain between Marri camps further magnify these effects. It is in such a situation, then, that the technique of imposed canalization of vertical communication becomes effective as a technique for the political dominance of a widely dispersed and economically independent population of commoners by a small and scattered elite.

The discussion so far has concentrated on the higher echelon leaders with seats in the central tribal council. The same general considerations affect the position of mutabars, the leaders of smaller subsections, and some wadera lines that have no seat in the council. The Marri can conceive of no group without a formal leader, and there are rules of etiquette (cf. pp. 72 f.) that call forth leaders whenever a collective acts, however temporarily, as a unit. But such positions of leadership are empty titles unless their incumbents succeed in canalizing through themselves all the crucial communications in question, particularly those with leaders of higher rank, which can be done successfully only by claiming and exercising the rank of leader—through the overt signals of being hospitable, owning a good horse, dressing well, constructing a permanent winter hut, exhibiting skill and grace in etiquette, observing Ramadan fast, and particularly by conspicuously mixing and communicating with leaders of higher rank and proving acceptable to them. Such men are sought by commoners as intermediaries and buffers between themselves and the influential leaders. They are also called on by commoners to pass judgment on minor disputes in ad hoc councils of three or four members— on some of which Pehrson was also asked to sit toward the end of his fieldwork.

Finally, each camp has its leader (*halk-waja*), a position that is allocated by mixed criteria of seniority and lineal descent, and competence. The wife of this leader (*godi*) is also ascribed a formal position as the leading woman of the camp. A proper understanding of these positions, however, presupposes an understanding of camp composition and organization, a subject that will be taken up later.

The terms "rank," "noble," "elite," and "caste" have figured in the preceding discussion of Marri sections and leaders. Such aspects of stratification clearly have a very intimate connection with political organizations, both as principles for ascribing political statuses and as sources of influence and effective power whereby authority and leadership may be exercised. Without giving analytic precedence to either the formal political system or the system of overall stratification, it is important to note the way in which they articulate, that is, the way in which the major division lines in the Marri system of stratification correspond to significant distinctions in the political system.

Traditional rates of compensation to be paid for wrongful killings offer a convenient index of this overall system of rank, since in them the Marris have been obliged to systematize their notions of inequality on a single scale, expressed in money and not in the idioms of social transactions, which also involve direct authority. The Marri tribal council recognizes a graded scale of blood compensation for men, running as follows:

	Rupees
Sardar, or other member of dynastic lineage (Bahawalanzai)	8,000
Waderas, mukadams, motabar-e-mard (other prominent men)	7,000–4,000
Kaum-e-mard (Marri commoners)	2,000
Seyyal (Pathan, Brahui, Baluch tribesman)	2,000
Kamin/kum-asil (Pathan serfs, Lori, Domb, and Jatt)	1,000
Mareta (slaves)	1,000

As for women, the rate of compensation for ordinary Marri women is Rs. 1,000, and for the families of higher-rank persons more, to be established by the council in each case.

The important gross distinctions are between (1) the noble leaders, (2) the bulk of the ordinary commoners—free men of Marri and other tribes, and (3) despised groups and persons. The distinctions between nobles and commoners is based in the final instance on the presence of titles—titles that, as shown above, ideally are vested in senior lines but that, to varying extent, may also be achieved through effective political activity and leadership. Within the commoner group there are thus great differences in rank, between poor, unsuccessful junior brothers in junior lines and wealthy, successful men who may have made themselves independent in such a way as to have a claim of seniority with respect to some order of grouping, who exercise leadership, have contact with nobles, and have aspirations to build up or be given a title for themselves. Until this ambition is achieved, they would probably, in the categorical context of blood compensation, fall into the commoner group, but in daily social life there is a border zone in which this differentiation is far from clear.

The distinction between commoners and members of the despised groups seems to be rather more clear in the everyday context. The lowest stratum is composed of a number of distinct and mostly clearly defined groups; their lower rank is continually confirmed in the etiquette of social intercourse and, for several of the groups, also by clear ethnic and cultural characteristics. An implication of their low rank is that it is dishonorable for a Marri to rob, threaten, or kill them; as a result they may wander rather freely, joining stranger camps for indefinite periods or just eating there and moving on. The most important despised groups that are individually or collectively tied to the Marri tribe and form a traditional part of the Marri social machinery are Hindu traders; various lineage fragments of Pashto-speaking serfs, Loris, Dombs, and Jatts; and slaves.

The position and role of the Hindko-speaking Hindu traders have been sketched above (p. 11). Present only periodically, and with their families resident outside the Marri area, they maintain a special and clearly distinct status, emphasized further by their deviant religion, dress, and native language. Yet they are an integral part of the Marri economic system and have certain rights to political protection through their special clientage contracts with local leaders. The Pehrson notes give no indication of the price paid in the event of compensation for the murder of a Hindu, but I assume it to be Rs. 1,000.

Of the Pashto-speaking tenants resident in the Marri area, only some fall in the despised *kamin/kum asil* category, whereas most are regarded as *seyyal*—unrelated equals. The despised tenants, whom we may call "serfs," are in the village of Badra reputed to be the descendants of the serfs of the previous Pathan rulers of Badra, while the non-despised Pathan tenant commoners are the supposed remnants of formerly dominant tribes. Intermarriage between Marris and the latter is infrequent but not dishonorable. In the case of a marriage between a Marri man and a *kamin* Pathan serf, on the other hand, the offspring will be given no rights in the father's agnatic section. A Marri woman will not be given in marriage to a Pathan serf.

Loris (Gypsies, smiths) and Dombs (musicians) are categories not very readily distinguishable from each other but clearly distinct from other groups. They are different from the Marris in details of custom and in their willingness to perform various kinds of degrading work, such as tinkering and playing music for money. Smithing and carpentry are also traditional Lori occupations, though, with the increasing opportunities resulting from larger sedentary communities, some Marri commoners have also taken up these professions. Lori and Domb women do not observe purdah and apparently often serve as prostitutes.

For these various reasons, Loris and Dombs are looked down upon; they are "like animals" (*mala-kār*) and are made to bear the brunt of a certain amount of crude jesting. Many families of them are attached specifically to a tribal section, which implies an obligation on their part to do menial work when called on, but also the right to request food or foodstuffs, nearly outworn objects of clothing, etc.—not simply as begging (which they also do) but as requests which the members of the particular section have an obligation to fulfill. Loris also often work as tenants and sometimes as shepherds for sedentary, wealthy Marris, and they are specialists in breaking, training, and shoeing horses. Though Lori and Domb women are sometimes married by Marris, the issue of such marriages are without rights in the Marri tribe, and Marri women are never given in marriage to Loris or Dombs. Though Baluchi-speaking, they are generally regarded as ethnically distinct and are identified with groups and castes of similar name and position in Persia, the Indus Valley, and northwestern India.

Jatts occupy a rather similar position and are sometimes loosely referred to as Loris, though they are, properly speaking, members of a non-Baluch-speaking population in Sindh and southwestern Panjab. Jatts among the Marris are mainly camel-herders and wandering peddlers, though they may also work as tenants, musicians, etc. Their political position depends on the bonds of clientship they establish with employers, camps, or section leaders.

Finally, there is the category "slave." Slavery is a traditional aspect of Baluch social organization, and though it never seems to have been very important among the Marris it was not abolished in all parts of the Marri area until 1952. Slaves seem to fall into two groups. Some slaves (*ti*) stem from Afghanistan, mostly Hazaras who were captured during the Afghan conquest of Hazarajat in the nineteenth century and brought in and sold to Marris by the Afghan nomads. Second, there are the Mareta, a small population with a (quasi) ethnic identity of their own, but associated with the Marri and owned by them, particularly by their leaders. According to local tradition, they are the descendants of prisoners captured by Mahmoud of Ghazni (*ca.* A.D. 1000) and given to the Baluch in return for their military support. All the aides de camp of the Marri sardars used to be Maretas, and their role in serving the sardar seems to have been the rather important one of replacing the sardar's collaterals (and dangerous rivals) as his confidants, and the Marri commoners (with section loyalties) as his bodyguards, while also providing domestic staff for menial and degrading services. Likewise, on a smaller scale, other important leaders kept slaves for such purposes. Of late, the main interest has been in owning female slaves, as concubines and servants.

The right to own slaves was not a noble prerogative; the limitation was merely the economic one of their relatively high price. Several owners could even own one slave jointly—"one leg each." Slave women were also married—to a slave, or even to a freeman, but not to the owner, who would have sexual access to her anyway and whose rights over her by Islamic law would be compromised if he were to marry her.

After emancipation the slaves were classed by the tribal council with other despised groups as regards rates of blood compensation; likewise, adultery by a commoner with a married Mareta woman cannot be punished by revenge killing, but only by beating and a compensation claim.

Society among the Marris is thus subdivided into three main strata: a middle stratum of commoners, constituting the vast majority of the population, an upper elite of title-holders, and a lower group of low-castes, serfs, and emancipated slaves. Full political status is given only to males of the upper two strata: they are organized in a comprehensive system of sections and subsections, associated with corporate estates in land, and joint political and legal responsibilities. Women and minors of these strata are the wards of the male head of their household; persons of the lower stratum may be tied by individual contracts to such freeman patrons or by collective contracts to sections, while some are essentially unattached and without political rights other than those that spring from a vague submission to Marri tribal institutions as a whole.

Section membership is ascribed through patrilineal descent but may be changed by subsequent political contract. With each section and subsection are associated one or several titles, the holders of which lead and represent the units in question. Some of the titles are transmitted according to strict principles of patriliny and seniority, others by mixed criteria of descent and achievement. The whole population is welded into a single, centralized political unit by allegiance to a single sardar, the holder of the highest title, and by acceptance of the authority of a central tribal council composed of the most important title-holders. The Marri themselves like to visualize their tribal system as a military organization based on a central supreme commander and composed of divisions and regiments with echelons of leaders.

Though this formal structure is very real and has great relevance to the lives of Marri commoners, it does not alone provide the predominant bases of Marri social structure. The life that unfolds in the tiny, dispersed, and shifting Marri camps derives its regularity from other factors as well, notably those relating to kinship. An understanding of these factors is a necessary basis for the understanding of Marri social life, and in the next chapter I shall try to abstract them from the empirical data in the forms of "a kinship system." Only after that has been done will I change the analytic focus from abstracted "systems," such as political organization and kinship, to an attempt to exhibit the structure of Marri society in the full context of the social life of the community.

IV

KINSHIP

THIS CHAPTER presents data on the kinship system, starting with a conventional chart that represents the consanguineal referential terminology of the Marri Baluch. In discussing these and other terms of relevance to kinship, including terms of address, the presentation moves from a phenomenological level toward a more systematic analysis. The behavioral characteristics of the main kinship relations will be described, and descriptions and generalizations of kinship terminology by Marris themselves will be used in order to identify the principles on which the classification of kin is based.

Certain such principles emerge clearly, notably those of generation, sex, and degree of collaterality, which provide the basis for a number of terminological discriminations. The descent principle, on the other hand, emerges with less clarity. Patrilineal descent is certainly of profound significance to the structure of the terminology, as one might expect in a society based largely on males and the male line, yet there seems to be ambiguity with respect to a range of categories that we would distinguish as agnates, consanguines, and affines. Though the criteria for such distinctions are clearly present and utilized, the weight given them in the classification of different relatives varies greatly, and they are usually combined—one is almost tempted to say confounded—with the criterion of sex. Thus for some purposes it seems as if *only* agnatic relationship is regarded as "real" kinship, and perhaps even Sister and Daughter are wholly within the fold, while Mother may be treated as a kind of affine. Yet, for other purposes, descent through male and female line is not distinguished, as in the term for "grandchild" and the term that denotes BrSoCh, BrDaCh.

Nor does it help to abandon analytic concepts such as agnate and affine, and try to use Marri discriminations, such as kinsman vs. stranger, own vs. MoBr's lineage, or their concepts of descent, lineage, "milk," and "male urine" as the basis for a schema of the logical components of Marri kinship terminology. An investigation of the use of such concepts in Marri discourse reveals that they lack analytic precision, in that different informants use them differently, and that their use, furthermore, relates to a number of criteria *outside* the field of kinship, such as structurally variable facts of residence, factional alignment, etc.

Toward the end of the chapter an incomplete componential analysis of the terminology is attempted in order systematically to show up these ambiguities in the principles underlying the terminology. It is suggested that these logical "inconsistencies" are not the artifacts of the conventional anthropological categories employed in the schema but represent a real conceptual ambivalence among the Marri, which springs from fundamental dilemmas in Marri culture, the most important of which concerns the position of women in Marri life. This theme will be further developed in the subsequent chapter on marriage.

The following data on kinship were obtained through the usual genealogical method, by hearing terms spoken in daily life, by abstract discussion, and by eliciting terms by posing kinship conundrums of the "if so-and-so had a son . . ." type. A continual difficulty was caused by the vagueness of knowledge of even the closest genealogical connections, except for the knowledge by the men of their patrilineal ancestors. Thus few persons know the name of their MoFa, while most men known that of their FaFaFaFa. This limited genealogical knowledge follows directly from characteristic features of Marri life: the smallness and isolation of local groups, the segregation of women, virilocalism, and the very young marriage age of females. A great deal of confusion is also generated by the high frequency of FaBrDa marriage, whereby ascendants and collaterals come to occupy several different kinship positions simultaneously, and accident or unexpressed rules of precedence determine the particular terms used. When pressed for information, informants would refer to senior persons, either genealogically or politically, as the ones who understand the system: "The old men know this—we don't. . . . Ask chief N. N., he knows such things. I am only a commoner."

A number of terms designating whole categories are used in discourse to differentiate kin from non-kin, but, because of the relativity of these terms, they cannot be used for analytical purposes to define the outer limits of kinship. *Kaum* ("nation," "caste") can denote various levels of predominantly endogamous groups, and thus the potential limits of kinship. But the term is also used in kinship contexts in the more abstract meaning of logical class or category (cf. citation, p. 42). An important opposition around which much kinship discussion revolves is that between *wati* and *seyyal*, with the respective connotation of "relative" vs. "unrelated social equal." Marriage is by preference with kin (i.e., *wati*), while *seyyal* are strangers and enemies, but, being equals, they are potentially marriageable, and through intermarriage they would be transformed into *wati*.

The terms *jind* and *aziz* are used for "relatives" collectively, implying or connoting some degree of patrilineal relationship. *Jind* (literally, "one's own") generally is used to distinguish "real" relatives from distant or classificatory ones, as in the phrase "my own Fa Br Ch" (*mai jind i nakozakht*).

Aziz refers to a broader group than *jind* and can have the general connotation of friend/kinsman, though, like *jind*, it may be opposed to *seyyal*. Especially by women, *aziz* may also be used for exclusively matrilaterally related persons, if they are close, while distant patrilineal relatives are, in some contexts, referred to as *seyyal*, even by male informants. For both these terms, as for the widest term, *wati*, there is clearly no unchanging criterion of genealogical distance by which one can define the boundaries of inclusion. For this reason, an understanding of the kinship system cannot begin from a discussion of its boundaries but must work outward from a central ego toward the periphery. This I shall do through a discussion of the terms as diagrammed in the accompanying Chart A, meanwhile qualifying the inevitable appearance of precision that is given.

The primary terms for Fa (*pith*), Mo (*math*), Br (*brath*), Si (*gwar*), So (*bāch*), Da (*jānik*), are not problematical. *Pith*, *math*, and *brath* have the dialect variants *pis*, *mas*, and *bras*. *Bāch* and *jānik* also mean "body" and "girl." Only primary relatives of the appropriate category are referred to by these terms. Uterine half-siblings may be specified as *math-e-brath*, *math-e-gwar*. Stepfather is called *pātrak*, mother's co-wife *ama*.

All other consanguineal kin terms may be used in an extended sense, usually in a classificatory manner for patrilineal collaterals of the relative but also sometimes by lineal extension. When it is of interest, the Marri differentiate these usages of the terms by contrasting *hakein* ("duty," real) vs. *waldein* ("distant"), *sākein* ("strong")/*pelin* ("line")/*khāse* ("proper") vs. *dir-e* ("far").

In the grandparental generation, FaFa (*dada*) and FaMo (*dadi*) are differentiated from MoFa (*nana*) and MoMo (*nani*) (var. Powadhi dialect: *nano*) but are classified with FaFaBr and FaFaBrWi, respectively. However, the dichotomization of FaFa/MoFa will frequently disappear, as in a reported conversation in which an informant cross-quizzed Pehrson on his understanding of the system: "What is *Nana?*" "Mother's father." "No, we call mother's father *Dada*." The reason for this confusion lies (in the case of this particular informant and also in general) in the effects of FaBrDa marriage and the extension of the term *Dada* to FaFaBr, who is also MoFa (cf. Fig. 4).

FIGURE 4

FaBr is *Baba* or *Babu*, as is also FaFaBrSo. The two forms seem to be interchangeable, though some informants claimed *Baba* to mean the real father's brother, *Babu* the classificatory father's brother, while others claimed Babu to be primarily referential and Baba vocative. The term *Chacha*, reportedly of Sindhi origin, is also frequently used for FaBr, and FaBrWi is usually referred

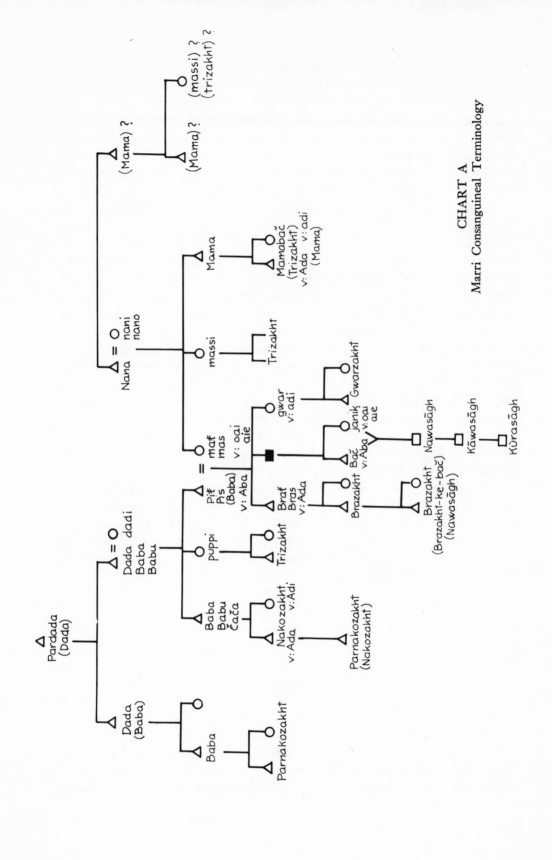

CHART A

Marri Consanguineal Terminology

to as *chachi*. In addition, the terms *Baba/Babu* are frequently extended to Fa, FaFaBr, both referentially and vocatively (for a discussion of vocative terms, see below, p. 46), to include all senior men of the lineage.

FaBr is differentiated from MoBr, who is *Mama*. *Mama* is also used for MoFaBrSo and, further, for any man belonging to the mother's lineage, clan, or tribe, if not otherwise related. Finally, *Mama* is used vocatively by Marris to Pathans and vice versa. "In the old days we Marris had a *Dada* and the Pathans had a *Dada*. One was a *Mama* and the other was a sister's son. Now since neither Marri nor Pathan know which was which, each addresses the other as *Mama*. Our *mamakhel* [mother's-brother lineage] are our *seyyal* [unrelated stranger]."

FaSi (*pupi*) is differentiated from MoSi (*masi*), and both terms may be extended to collaterals of the same generation within their respective lineages. Cousin terms are illustrated in the accompanying chart, B. Agnatic first cousins are called *nakozakht*, and agnatic second cousins are grouped with male agnatic first cousin's children as *par nakozakht*; the latter may also be called *nakozakht* by lineal extension from their father. *Nakozakht* are differentiated from *Trizakht*, covering all other actual or classificatory cousins.[1] Distinctions within this category specify the nature of the linkage by compound terms: FaSiCh is called *Pupibach* (males) or *Pupichuk* (both sexes), while MoBrCh is referred to as *Mamabach* and *Mamachuk*. MoSiCh may be described as *Massibach* and *Massichuk*, but are generally referred to as *Trizakht*, and the relationship is not important. Non-agnatic second cousins are regarded as very distant relatives indeed, but would on occasion be described as *waldein* (distant) *Trizakht*, if not clearly identified with mother's lineage, when they would be called *Mama*. Members of mother's lineage are collectively and singly referred to as *mamakhel*, and, by lineal extension, all such males may be addressed as *Mama*. Sister's children and their offspring are *gwarzakht*; brother's offspring are *brazakht*. BrSoCh may also be classified with own grandchildren (SoCh and DaCh) as *nawasagh*. Terms for further descending generations—somewhat hypothetical and not widely known—are *kawasagh* (own ChChCh and BrSoSoCh) and *kurasagh* (own ChChChCh and BrSoSoSoCh).

The main structural principles of this terminological system seem to be generation, patrilineage, and sex. With the addition of rank, they are also the variables of far greatest importance in structuring all interpersonal relationships and behavior among the Marri. But in the kinship terminology none of these principles is followed through systematically, and they are conceptualized and combined in various ethnographically specific ways that remain to be discussed. The main dilemma of this discussion, and I believe of the Marris' conceptualization, is that of the position of the women: the extent to which they are given agnatic

1. It may be of some etymological interest that the suffix *-zakht* indicates "born of," and *Naku* is used as a term of address interchangeably with *Baba*, while an informant from Persian Mekran gave the terms *Naku* for FaBr and *Tru* for MoBr, MoSi, and FaSi.

status, the extent to which they are assimilated into their husband's groups, and the nature of the relationship between a mother and her children. Until, at a later stage, I take up specifically the differences between the male and female views of the system, I shall discuss these questions from the male point of view, but this reservation means less than it might, since with one exception in the affinal terminology to be given below, all formal terminology is identical for male and female speakers.

Looking outward from the position of an ego, the classification of relatively close kin that this terminology provides seems to be open to interpretations of different kinds; the bases for the classification might variously be interpreted as lineage, bifurcation, or sex. I shall try to describe the forms given by the Marri to such conceptualizations and the contexts in which they deem them relevant.

Several alternative modes of conceptualization are connected with the crucial dichotomization of the father's, or male, side (*palavar, tāk*) and the mother's or female, side. One basis for this dichotomy is expressed in an axiom of Marri

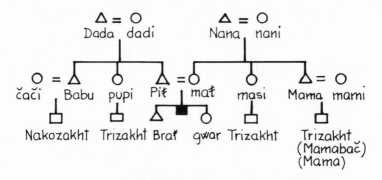

CHART B
Cousin and Uncle/Aunt Terms

kinship: "My share is on my father's side; on my mother's side there is nothing [*Pith e palvara mai wānd āst; math a palavar hechi nist*]." This is the view that articulates kinship, descent, and the tribal system, and I shall return to it shortly. But there is also another possible conceptualization, utilizing the word *tāk*, which can have the sense of "a *piece* of cloth," or "today you will visit the women's *section*." Thus, informants may speak of kin on the mother's side as *math-e-tāk*, suggesting a concept of bifurcation. A residual cognatic term not yet discussed may have its place here. The notes contain only two explanatory statements on it:

"*Niaghi*: relationship on the mother's side. My sister or other distant relatives—any woman having relationship to me: my daughter. One to whom I give a shawl upon engagement." "*Niaghi*: persons to whom I give a shawl or any kind of cloth when attending my own or my son's marriage. When they depart after the wedding ceremony I put the cloth on their head. [P: although this was done in the case I saw by the oldest female relative of the groom. Thus *niaghi* are distant and female relatives, sisters, or any relationship on the side of mother. Daughters.]"

This classifying of female maternal relatives together with own sisters and daughters, rather than any stringent concept of bifurcation, seems to be characteristic of Marri notions. The relevant distinction is not so much between maternal and paternal relatives as between agnates who perpetuate the agnatic relationship, that is, males, contrasted to other relatives. Yet some concept of bifurcation must have led one informant in a discussion to claim *math-e-tāk* to be *trizakht* and *pupibach* to be *nakozakht*, that is, MoBrCh + MoSiCh vs. FaBrCh + FaSiCh. This type of confusion will be augmented by cases of FaBrDa marriage, where FaSi has married FaFaBrSo (cf. Fig. 5). It was countered by other Marris by the argument that FaSiCh inherits his father's group affiliation and hence is another line and not a *nakozakht*, and "you can't be both *nakozakht* and *mamakhel*."

FIGURE 5

Another way of conceptualizing paternal and maternal relations emerges in a discussion of incest (*naravā*, literally: "no going"). "There are two things you must avoid: one is father's urine, the other is mother's milk. A man and his son's urine is the same. A woman and her sisters have the same milk." The invariant connection between these injunctions and the forbidden degrees remains somewhat unclear; some of the reason for it may be that koranic marriage regulations are in fact applied by religious practitioners, though only imperfectly known in the Marri population. Lay informants agreed that the following are *naravā*: Mo, SoWi, FaSi, MoSi, Si, Da. In addition, if adultery (*siakhar*, cf. pp. 65 ff.) is committed with the following, this too is *naravā*: FaWi, BrWi, FaBrWi; but these women may be married if widowed (though a mullah would refuse to perform a wedding between a man and his widowed FaWi). Intercourse with MoBrWi is adultery and sin, but not *naravā*. "She belongs to another group [*kaum*]."

The important contrast between milk and urine is the emphasis on laterality in the former and lineality in the latter. The idiom of urine is used for patrilineage in a number of contexts (cf. p. 81), though without being capable of demarcating collateral limits. The notion of common milk, however, is clearly limited to relations of filiation and can never span more than one generation in depth or extend laterally beyond a sibling group.

The qualitative difference in the social content of agnatic and uterine relationships is expressed in the contrast between *haqi* and *nahaqi*, "duty" and "nonduty." Only sons of the same father are "duty" brothers (*haqi brath*), whereas sons of one mother from different fathers are terminologically brothers to each other, but in relationship that is *nahaqi* and implies no invariant rights and duties but only an expectation of familiarity and mutual decency toward each other.

It would seem that the only invariant framework of rights and duties, of "real" kin relations, is that of patrilineage. The importance of patriline as a component in the terminological system is apparent in cousin terms, in the terminology for mother's agnates, in affinal terms (cf. the accompanying chart, C:

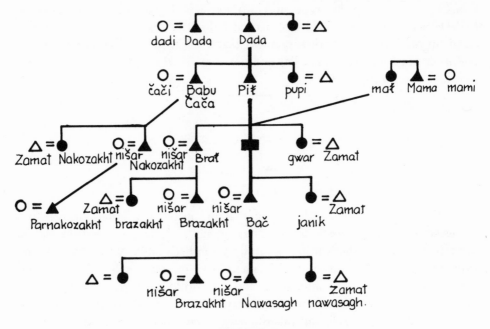

CHART C
Affines of Consanguines

Affines of Consanguines), and also in the way a number of terms are extended. Lineal groupings can also be expressed by the suffix *-khel* (patrilineal descent group); Marri informants prefer to discuss more distant collaterals in terms of such undifferentiated collectivities as *mamakhel* (MoBr, MoBrSo, MoSi, MoFa-BrSo, etc.), *nanakhel* (MoFa, MoFaBr, MoFaSi, etc.), *nanikhel* (MoMo, Mo-MoBr, MoMoSi, MoMoBrSo, etc.), or *dadikhel* (FaMo, FaMoBr, FaMoSi, FaMoBrSo, etc.).

The basic patrilineal unit is the *waris* or minimal lineage. Always included are agnatic first cousins. Again, high frequency of FaBrDa marriage enables informants to think of such a group as including all or most close kin:

"*Waris* are FaBr, FaBrSo, BrChi, Fa, So, FaFa, ChiChi. Also included are SiChi, if they are near." P: "What do you mean?" "If you give your sister to somebody far then the children will not be near, but if given to FaBrSo as we have just given Addi to Abdullah, then sister's children become *waris*, for they are both *nakozakht* and *gwarzakht*."

Other concepts for descent group are *rānd* ("line," also "custom," "way"), *jind* ("one's own"), *khanadan* ("pure-blooded family," "aristocracy").

The minimal lineage shares jural responsibility for blood revenge and for punishing adultery; they are also the heirs to all private property held by members. But in both these fields of rights they are graded in terms of lineal and collateral distance, somewhat differently for the two purposes. Rights to property and to legal guardianship over women and minors pass upon the death of a man to his *waris* in the following order, with the presence of a nearer agnate excluding the more distant from a share: So—SoSo—Fa—Br—BrSo—FaFa—FaBr—FaBrSo—FaFaFa or his descendants—men of the patrilineal section (*tākār mard*). The duty or right to avenge a death and, more importantly, to kill an unfaithful wife and her lover, when her husband fails to do so himself, passes to

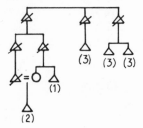

FIGURE 6

members of the dead man or husband's *waris* in the following order: Br—Fa and So—FaBrSo—FaBr, and no further. However, some informants state the rights of FaBr to precede FaBrSo, doubtless involving a compromise between degree of agnatic nearness, as expressed in the order of inheritance, and the degree of involvement and assertiveness, greater in young adult than in senior and aged generations.

The notion of descent is clearly coupled with one of segmentation and degrees of collateral distance, valid throughout in terms of the dichotomy of near vs. distant and expressed in the terminological distinctions between Br, FaBrSo, and FaFaBrSoSo. For purposes of inheritance, descending generations are consistently regarded as being closer than ascendants, so a BrSo is closer than a FaBr. In a particular case of marriage guardianship for a widow, the following order of precedence was defined: first, the widow's Br; second, No. 2, not *qua* widow's or dead husband's son, but since he is the woman's FaBrSoSo; the actual leaders of the camp in question come only third, being FaFaBrSos and thus common agnatic descendants of a more distant agnate than is No. 2 (cf. Fig. 6).

Other statements, explicating the principles of kinship, proceed from a notion of the basic unity of a line and see its growth through time as the basis for allocating pride of place to relatives. Thus: "A man has three close kin categories. First of all, there is FaFa, then Fa, then there is oneself. . . . Their children are close. Beyond that, everyone else is distant. Look at Domar—he is my BrSo but he is already distant [*Marduma sai nazikh-e-kaum āst. Sari sari Dada e; guda pith; guda tau e*".] A similar ordering of generations was made of mother's agnates, with the added difficulty of fitting in the mother—a mere woman, yet the manifest link with the group—into the order of nearness: "Of mother's relatives there are three groups: your own mother's parents, your own mother's siblings, the offspring of your mother's siblings. Beyond this everything is distant. Mother's relatives are in the following order of relationship to you: MoFa, Mo, MoBr, MoBrCh." However, in the case of maternal relatives, the question of segmentation and increasing distance between collaterals is not considered, since it is irrelevant to ego.

Agnatic relationship takes precedence over other kin relationships. Cases were observed in which small children, accepting their mother's usage, were cor-

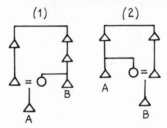

FIGURE 7

rected by their fathers and instructed to use agnatic terms. Thus in Figure 7, case (1) A may call B *Mama* when speaking to him, but was made to refer to B as my *parnakozakht* (FaFaBrSoSo). Similarly, in case (2) A refers to B as his *nakozakht* or *parnakozakht* (FaBrSoSo), though he might use *gwarzakht* (SiSo) vocatively.

The predominance given to the male line in kinship also implies certain notions about the basic relationships in the triangle Fa, Mo, and Ch. The questions at issue here are the interconnections of marriage, descent, and the male/female dichotomy. They are best understood through a discussion of the status of the woman. A woman clearly is not given full membership in her natal agnatic group—she has no rights to its estate and no recognized voice in its deliberations. The marriage contract transfers authority and responsibility over the woman from the marriage guardian (her closest agnate) to the husband, in return for a bride-price. The husband's agnates may share somewhat in these rights and responsibilities, as we have seen in the case of adultery punishment. Yet the woman is not incorporated into her husband's group, not even in the shadowy "female" capacity. If the husband dies, the widow's remarriage is arranged by her closest agnate and there is no levirate, and the bride-price for the second marriage goes in full to her agnates. Emotionally, a woman always continues to identify herself with her natal group; the "home" of a married woman is her father's tent.

When a woman is discovered in adultery, and her husband's minimal lineage fails to exact punishment, the dormant interests of her natal group are recognized in her brother's—alternatively, father's—right to punish. On the other hand, the ambiguous position of a married woman—virtually abandoned by her own group, yet not assimilated as a member in that of her husband—is illustrated by the indecision as to who shall receive the bride-price for women *divorced* because of adultery. Such women were traditionally sold, either out of Marri territory altogether or at least out of their former husband's section;[2] by various precedents, the bride-price may go to the tribal chief, or half to the chief and half to her relatives, or one-third each to the section chief, her relatives, and her husband.

Other ambiguities emerge if one looks at the relationship between the children and their mother. The social identity of children is clearly determined by their *agnatic* descent. In important contexts, children seem to regard even their own mother as a kind of affine:

"My brother and I were very young when my father died. My mother stayed 3 months in the home of the father of her dead husband, then went to her own home for 9 months. Then her father arranged for her to be married to another man. We stayed with her until we became bigger, making occasional visits to our own FaFa's home; and then we came to live with our FaBr [*Baba*]. We said to our mother: 'We are not your children, we are our *Baba's* children, and our home is there.' "

On the other hand, that is not the only possible view. The special tie between Mo and Ch is recognized in the terminology, where she is not merely FaWi, for stepmother (*ama*) is distinguished from own mother (*math*).[3] Furthermore, the social position of children is modified by that of their mother: children of low-caste mothers are not given full tribal status (they are not *khanadan*), though such marriages are true marriages that have the same legal form as any other marriage, and there is no question as to the legitimacy of the child. Rather,

2. The practice of selling adulterous women outside the tribe was prohibited by recent legislation by the tribal council, legislation designed to discourage husbands from divorcing their wives through (false) adultery accusations by assuring that the accusing husband will not be able to recoup his bride-price. Traditional customs gave the wronged husband the bride-price paid for his wife on her remarriage, though it gave him no influence as to *whom* his divorced wife should be married to.

3. The stepmother term looks linguistically like the vocative terms, but the notes clearly designate it as referential, *aiye* (Mo) as vocative usage to stepmother. Notes from an early phase of fieldwork also mention *mattin* as a term for mother's co-wife; this may be correct, or it may be an error derived from the term *mattin brath* for agnatic half-brothers.

this declassing of the children of low mothers derives from the Marri recognition of the bilaterality of biological connections. The inheritance of character traits from both parents is implicit in myths, for example:

"The Prophet engaged his daughter Bibi to four men. Time passed and they all four appeared asking for his daughter's hand in marriage. So the Prophet took a bitch who was lying nearby and with a big *bismillah* ["in the name of God"] turned it into a likeness of his daughter. Then he took a female donkey and did the same. Then he took a nearby cow, and did the same. To one of the men he gave his own daughter, but no one knows which one. Now when you see a person who is always lying and cursing, you know his grandmother was probably that bitch. Or one that is lazy and insolent, his grandmother was probably a donkey. Only a fourth of us are pure humans. But no one knows which is which."

In summary, the relations in the triangle Fa, Mo, and Ch are not structured solely by a simple dichotomy of agnatic descent vs. affinal tie; although this is very important, it is modified by a fundamentally bilateral view of kinship. But the expression of this view is always affected by the dichotomization of male and female and the associated, very marked differentiation of the kinds of relationships that one can have to them respectively. Thus, while mother and close matrilateral relatives are more than mere affines, father's sister and own sister are less than proper agnates and are, rather, peripheral and nonessential relatives in the same way as are matrilateral relatives. The assimilation of all these relatives into one category is illustrated in the term *niaghi* discussed above (p. 38).

It is also expressed in a characteristic, though incorrect, statement of one informant discussing terminology: "The women of my mother's brother's lineage [*Mamakhel*] are nothing to me—or perhaps they are SiCh [*gwarzakht*]"—a mistake not based on a misplaced reciprocal usage but arising out of the female sex in the connecting link, making them "quasi"-kin.

It is hardly surprising that with such views of the role of kinship through males and through females should go clear differences in the interpretations of the kinship system by men and by women. The preceding discussion has expounded the male view as the canonical view of how the terminology should be used and of the components of meaning that are implied. Women share the same terminological system as men; it is only in certain features of the use and the extension of the terms, and in the view of kinship that they see expressed in these terms, that they may be seen to differ somewhat. Women place more importance on female relatives and female links, and their view of kinship comes nearer to embracing a bilateral kindred. When multiple relations exist, agnatic terms do not necessarily take precedence over cognatic. Likewise, in female use the terms *kaum* and *aziz* are extended to include matrilateral relatives clearly excluded in the male view. In a case in which husband and wife were related as matrilateral parallel cousins, the husband said that his wife was not an *aziz* but a *seyyal* ("stranger"), whereas she claims to be married to an *aziz*. The relative equivalence, in the female view, of patri- and matrikinship is also revealed by their view of half-siblings. An otherwise excellent female informant insisted that *ḥaqi brath* ("duty" brothers) are only those of one father and one mother, while all half-siblings, whether agnatic or uterine, are *naḥaqi* ("non-duty").

"You have seen that my husband does not live with his two brothers. We live alone. The reason is that they are *naḥaqi*. My husband's stepmother never comes to see us at all. Also, once my husband was sick and went to his brother's home. They wouldn't try to make him well—didn't do anything. He has no *ḥaqi* brothers and sisters, for his mother had only one child."

The affinal terminology remains to be discussed. In it the lineal principle is most evident (cf. accompanying charts, C and D). In ascending generations, the

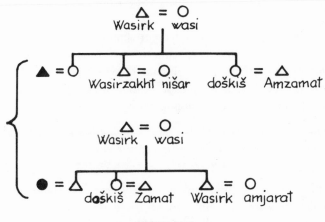

CHART D
Own Affines, Male/Female Speaking

wives of FaFaBr, FaBr, and MoBr are assimilated to their husbands' kinship positions and marked off from them by the feminine suffix -*i*. In own and descending generations, men who marry women of ego's minimal lineage are *Zamat*, as is HuSiHu, and the wives of men of the minimal lineage are *nishar*, as is WiBrWi. Own wife is *zal*, though the term is avoided and teknonymy or euphemistic use of "family" is preferred. Husband is *mard* ("man"). Special terms are used for spouse's Fa, Mo, Br, and Si; WiSiHu is *Amzamat* ("co-affine"), co-wife is *huffok*, HuBrWi is *amjarat*. None of the affinal terms are extended to their lineals or collaterals.

In different contexts, affinal relationship (*sangoband*) is variously described by informants as "meaning nothing" and as implying an aspect of kinship, though to a rather modest extent.

"When you become affinally related to someone, then it is God's command not to do badness or rottenness to them. If they are strangers [*seyyal*], then there is no duty, it does not matter if you steal or fight. But when they become affines, then there is law. . . . There are really no definite duties. But if you are going to do meritorious acts to someone, then you should do it to your affines."

Vocative terms show a different structure from the referential terms. Parent-child reciprocals are *Aba* (to males) and *oai* or *aiye* (to females); these may also be extended to stepparents and stepchildren, and to grandparents and grandchildren. Brothers and male cousins are classed together as *Ada;* sister, female cousin, and, for female speakers, co-wife, are called *adi.* *Mama*, MoBr, is used vocatively to senior men with whom one wishes to emphasize intimacy, though never to a senior agnate. *Baba* (senior agnate) is a term of greater respect. *Naku* is a frequent term of address to old men, also a term of respect to old women. High-status women may also be addressed as *Adi* ("brother"), while *pupi* (FaSi) is appropriate for senior women with whom one has relatively intimate contact.

A final principle of kinship organization should be noted, though it fails to find expression in the terminology, namely, lateral seniority by order of birth, through which elder brothers in the absence of senior generations assume authority over their juniors. The principle of primogeniture thus defines positions of authority and leadership in every sibling group.

"The elder brother has great authority. The younger brother should be his right-hand man. If the younger brother commits a wrong, the elder brother will say 'I did it.' If the younger brother performs a great act, the elder brother will get credit for it."

The classification of cognatic and affinal kin that the Marri referential terminology provides thus seems mainly to be based on a few, relatively pervasive, principles, which are conceptualized by the actors themselves and which are of the greatest importance to their behavior. But some of these conceptualizations are rather limited and ambiguous, and the principles that they purport to express seem in some respects to change their quality as they are applied in different sectors of the kinship terminology. To explore the extent of such an ambiguity, or variability in content, of the principles underlying the terminology, I shall attempt to construct a rigorous deductive schema with which the actual terminology may be compared and contrasted.[4] In other words, a componential model will be used, not to demonstrate a hypothecated consistency in the logical bases of the terminology, but to pinpoint and specify the areas of *in*consistency.

4. The following approximation to a componential analysis arises from certain suggestions in Pehrson's notes, as well as from the character of their contents, and is in line with his earlier treatment of Lappish kinship terminology (Pehrson 1957, esp. pp. 25–33). For its importance in enabling me to understand the implications of these incomplete and fragmentary suggestions, I wish to acknowledge my debt to Goodenough's (1956) explication of componential analysis. However, the blame for the obvious failure to emulate the methodological rigor of such analysis rests on myself and the particular circumstances of this effort and not on Pehrson.

My reading of the data presented in this chapter leads me to single out the following components as those most likely to produce a classification like that found in Marri kinship terminology: (1) mode of relationship: consanguine vs. affine, (2) lineality: agnate vs. non-agnate, (3) sex: male vs. female, (4) generation: —3 to +2. The Marri terminology does not make all the discriminations that would be produced by permutations of these components, but that does not reduce the model's usefulness. However, certain discriminations that *are* made in Marri kinship terminology, as between Br, FaBrSo, and FaFaBrSoSo, require an additional component, namely, (5) distance: distinction between lineal and collateral, and degrees of collaterality. The accompanying schematic chart locates most Marri kinship terms with reference to permutations of these components. For the sake of diagrammatic simplicity, some areas of permutation that do not find expression in Marri terminology have been ignored, that is, the sex distinction is disregarded for some of the terms in own and descending generation, and the distinctions of lineality and degree of collaterality are relevant only to agnates of first ascending, own, and first descending generation and to the distinction Mo/MoSi.

What interests us is the degree of fit between the chart and the Marri terminology—the extent to which Marri terminological classes correspond to those generated by permutations of these rigidly invariant five components. Though the overall fit is good, certain significant differences emerge very clearly at the points at which Marri terms do not correspond to the pigeonholes of the chart. Some of these cases are not very important, as for instance the lack of fit revealed in the clustering of terms for affines of own generation, which could be eliminated by the use of further components. Thus the *e*xclusion of WiBr and HuBr (*Wasirzakht*) and WiSi and HuSi (*doshkish*) from the categories containing SiHu and BrWi, which, however, *in*clude HuSiHu and WiBrWi, implies an additional distinction between spouse's consaguines and agnate's spouses, while a parallel sex principle seems to be relevant to the terms of WiSiHu (*Amzamat*) and HuBrWi (*amjarat*).

Much more importantly, one whole category of terms, best described as "wives of kinsmen of ascending generations," namely, FaMo, MoMo, FaBrWi, MoBrWi (*dadi, nani, chachi, mami,* respectively), emerges by default. It would seem that they are treated alike in a manner inconsistent with the componential model, as a kind of female affine assimilated to their husband's positions, that is, by dichotomization of "male" vs. "affine" with total disregard for other relevant components.

Nor does the schema show the possibility of describing MoBrSo as *Mama* and FaBrSoSo as *Nakozakht* by lineal extension. Finally, and again very significantly, the agnatic/non-agnatic dichotomy breaks down when applied to second descending generation.

As I understand them, these discrepancies between the componential model

MARRI KINSHIP TERMINOLOGY: INCOMPLETE COMPONENTIAL SCHEMA

Consanguine				Affine		
Agnate		Non-agnate				
Male	Female	Male	Female	Male	Female	Generations
Pardada						−3
Dada		Nana				−2
1: Pith 2: Baba	pupi	Mama	1: math c: masi	Wasirk	wasi	−1
c1: Brath ⎤ gwar c2: Nakozakht c3: Parnakozakht		Trizakht		Wasirzakht Zamat Amzamat	doshkish nishar amjarat	0
1: Bach ⎤ janik c1: Brazakht c2: Parnakozakht		Gwarzakht		Zamat	nishar	+1
1: Nawasagh c: Brazakht		Nawasagh Brazakht Gwarzakht		Zamat	nishar	+2

l = lineal; c = collateral, of var. degrees.

and the terminology demonstrate certain very important ethnographic facts. Most of the discrepancies can be traced back to one single issue: the position to be accorded to women as kinsfolk and agents of kinship. This is an issue on which there is genuine ambivalence emotionally and, I would claim, conceptually, among the Marri. Drawing on evidence presented in the previous pages, as well as that incorporated in the schema, one might say that on the issue of recognizing kinship through women three incompatible views compete, as follows:

1. For some purposes, it seems as if *only* agnatic relationships are recognized. Thus FaMo is classed as a kind of affine, as FaFaWi in a category with FaFaBrWi, and in a way analogous to FaBrWi (and MoFaWi). As we have seen, Mother is also sometimes conceptualized in this way (cf. p. 43), though not in the kinship terminology.

2. For other purposes, kinship through women—Mo, FaSi, Si, etc.—is the basis for the recognition of non-agnatic consanguines. This view is the one

adopted in the componential model, through which a number of important terms fall into place.

3. Finally, for some purposes even descent through women is recognized. Thus, own, brother's, and sister's *bilateral* descendants emerge as categories in the second descending generation, though as a kind of left-handed recognition of the agnatic principle BrSoCh may also be included among "own grandchildren"—probably only by male speakers.

The comparison of the terminology and the componential model thus serves to show up the inconsistencies in the Marri view of kinship through women. Once they have been so identified, the sociological reasons are readily apparent why Marri ambivalence in the recognition of women should express itself unequally through the generations. Second ascending generation presents itself to ego as clearly structured by patrivirilocal residence and male dominance. Female agnates of that generation have long since been married out, so there are no terms for them, and the women who are there are so by virtue of their marriage to senior men—that is, all women fall into place as wives of male kinsmen. This also holds for many women in first ascending generation. In ego's own and adjoining generations, on the other hand, the intimacies of domestic life and the continued identification of the mother with her own kin provide for contacts with a number of closer bilateral kinsfolk of both sexes. At the same time, the *distinction* between agnates and non-agnates is of overriding importance, since the content of kinship relations in these generations consists conspicuously of matters of politics and property. Finally, the second descending generation is of interest to ego only as distant offspring. They are children who have no political role vis-à-vis ego, who hold no property and will play no role in any relationship with ego outside the purely domestic sphere; therefore the distinction agnate/non-agnate recedes in importance.

It thus adds to the understanding of the terminological system to consider the situation, the social environment in which it is operative. Also, the question of the limits of kinship is then seen in a different perspective. Marri local groups are small, widely dispersed, and held apart by conflict and mutual suspicion. Residence is strongly patrivirilocal, a fact that, combined with early female marriage and severe restrictions on female intercommunication, gives room for an effective field of kinship relations of very limited scope. Add to this the involuting effect of frequent FaBrDa marriage, and the situation becomes even more extreme. Asked about the classification of more distant collaterals, informants were unsure and readily confused. A good informant, when asked what the term for mother's FaBrDa would be, answered, apparently correctly, that it "might be *masi* [MoSi] but then probably not anything. We use those terms in our household, but her we are not acquainted with." Actual limits of social intercourse set the effective limits of kinship terms and genealogical knowledge. This fact related very importantly to the introductory discussion of this chapter, where the limits of kinship were discussed with reference to distinction as that between *wati*, "kin," and *seyyal*, "stranger." This distinction is of central importance in a great deal of kinship discourse, but the limits of *wati* will be empirical rather than definitional and will thus necessarily have an agnatic bias. Besides, relativity and pulsations in the inclusiveness of the *wati* category will relate precisely to the purpose of the discourse: extensions and denials of kin loyalties and demands, ways of claiming rights or expressing suspicion and rejection vis-à-vis other persons or camps. Thus different texts vary, some asserting that even agnatic cousins are *seyyal*, some including whole (agnatic) tribal sections as *wati*.

Finally, the Marri ambivalence in the recognition of kinship through women can be clarified and better understood by considering the wider cultural syndrome—the dichotomization of the sexes—of which it is a part. Indeed, this dichotomy is given a content and relevance by the Marri that makes it fundamental to an understanding of a great deal of social life, as will be shown in later chapters. I shall here only indicate how categorical and comprehensive it is, and what its main themes are.

Men and women are regarded as basically different, and entirely different standards of evaluation are applied to them: men should show manliness (*mardi*); women are commended for modesty (*lajji*). Furthermore, the social life of the sexes is kept segregated, both in terms of actual frequency of interaction across sex boundaries and in terms of symbolic and explicit separations of the male and the female sphere. It is not merely a question of the purdah isolation of women from contact with the outside world and unrelated men. Among the Marri the observation of such purdah prevents all men beyond the limits of first cousin of the woman or her husband from having any social interaction with her, unless they, through some other equally intimate relationship, have been established as members of the household. But, even within these limits, interactions between the sexes are few and restricted. Every camp, no matter how small, has at least two campfires at night, around each of which only one sex congregates, and the same separation is expressed ceremonially in separate dancing circles for weddings and other festivals (among all Marris except Powadhis). There is an absolute ban on public commensality between the sexes, though lovers may eat together in secret. Except for ceremonial occasions, each man eats in his own tent, alone or with his unmarried sons, while the women of the family eat elsewhere in privacy or subsequently, when the men have left.

The relationship of brother and sister, on the other hand, is a close one, allowing for both deep attachment and considerable behavioral freedom. When others are not present, Br and Si will sit together at the same fire; they speak to each other about a variety of personal topics and are conventionally expected to be deeply concerned about each other's welfare. The relationship is also one that implies mutual influence—when Robert Pehrson was made ritual brother to a girl at her marriage, she later boasted to his wife that now she would be able to decide on matters concerning them, what Jean, as wife, was in no position to affect.

The dichotomy of the sexes is particularly dramatized in the husband-wife relationship, which is frequently represented by the informants as a relationship of structurally inevitable opposition and hostility. The ban on man-woman commensality is expanded to an absolute taboo against the husband's eating any food from which his wife has eaten or drinking any water from which she has drunk. The expected hostility and lack of identification between husband and wife, contrasted with the strong identification of father and son as men and closest agnates, are illustrated by the musings of a little nine-year-old orphan girl by the women's campfire one evening:

"One day my MoBrWi, who was also my Si, was sitting grinding flour. Her son was crying and she did not stop grinding to stop his crying—or perhaps she didn't even hear him. My MoBr came and hit her just over the back of the neck with his shepherd's crook. She fell unconscious on the grindstone and he walked away carrying his son."

The woman's attitude to marriage was summarized by one young, favorite wife:

". . . young or old, virgin or widow, a woman will not of her own volition get married. Her heart tells her that men are bad—she is afraid. But Pathan women of their own volition get husbands. . . . I had an age-mate once, my very best friend, a Pathan. One day she said: 'Now I shall tell my father that I wish he would try to find a husband for me.' I told her not to get married, that men were bad. But she insisted."

Thus the ambivalence in the recognition of kinship through women that is revealed in the analysis of the kinship terminology shows what is perhaps the most profound dilemma in Marri culture: women as wives and affines are strangers—as will be shown in more detail below, they are polluting and despicable—yet they are the source of the two most highly prized goods in Marri culture—sex and descendants. But women as kinsfolk and agnates, while they may be stripped of all rights and responsibilities, are still a man's sisters and daughters and can cause him honor and dishonor as close agnates.

Even with the support of such extraneous material as has been introduced in the preceding pages, the possibilities of explicating the structure of Marri society through a formal kinship analysis seem to be exhausted. A deeper understanding calls for an exploration of the consequences of the Marri male/female dichotomy, requiring the presentation of systematic data on the marriage transaction, and the organization of domestic life.

V

MARRIAGE AND THE RELATION
BETWEEN MAN AND WOMAN

*"FaFa Adam and FaMo Hawa gave birth one night to twins, a boy and a girl.
The second night, twins—a boy and a girl—again were born. Adam gave the
first-night girl to the second-night boy, and the second-night girl to the first-
night boy. He thus made woman-exchange [māttān] marriage between the two.
The third night, another set of twins was born. The boy born that night said:
'I do not want woman exchange. I want to marry my own sister.' And she
was given to him. The first two husbands said: 'Our descendants shall be Mos-
lems,' while the third said: 'Mine will be unclean because I married my sister;
mine will be infidels.' "*

MARRI NOMAD camps are so small that they encompass a unit of narrower
range than that of close kinship. Their organization can therefore be a
predominantly familial organization, that is, one in which roles and
relationships between persons have primary reference to kinship positions. In
the activities of groups thus organized, marriages must be transactions of prime
importance. In the present chapter I shall concentrate first on the marriage transaction itself, to show its jural content, and then describe the conjugal relations
of spouses, leading on to a discussion of Marri values and behavior connected
with sex and love.

Marriage among the Marri is, in agreement with Islamic law, a contract between men concerning the transfer of rights over a woman. The parties in such
contracts are, on the bride's side, her closest male agnate and thus typically her
father, while on the groom's side his closest senior male agnate or, in the relatively fewer cases of marriage by an adult man who is the head of his own
household, the groom himself. We thus normally need to distinguish three
parties to the transaction—the husband, his agnates, and the wife's agnates—and
we need to distinguish rights over the woman and rights over the issue of the
marriage.

Legal rights over the woman are vested in the husband, and in him alone, at
the completion of the marriage. She is bound to him personally, not to his agnatic line; nor do her agnates retain any active rights over her. The specific
nature of her relationship to her husband and not to his lineage is demonstrated

in the event of his death, when rights of disposal over her revert to her agnates, whether the marriage has been consummated or not. There is no practice of levirate and no compensation to anyone but her husband for damages caused to her. The only suggestion that her husband's agnates have rights over her is the rule that they may, in his place, punish adultery on her part (cf. p. 41), but "if the husband does not give permission, there can be no killing, because the husband owns the woman." I think the correct interpretation would be that his agnates are involved because his honor—in which his agnates share—will be damaged by a failure to punish, not because their rights have in any way been infringed by the act of adultery.

As for the total legal separation of the wife from her own agnates, that is demonstrated by a number of facts. A husband can refuse his wife permission to visit her agnates and can refuse them access to her if they seek out his camp and home. The notes contain a moving case history of a man who waited all night outside the compound of his village-dwelling sister to see her on her deathbed, being refused access to her by her husband until it was too late. Likewise, if a woman commits a murder, responsibility rests with her husband, not her agnates; only if she kills her husband—thereby becoming a widow—does responsibility revert to her own agnates.

These rights over the woman must be clearly distinguished from rights to the fruits of the marriage, that is, the question of legitimacy and guardianship over the children. In his exercise of paternal rights over his offspring, the husband stands not alone but as representative of his agnatic group, and, in the event of his death, his rights devolve on his collaterals, while the children, by virtue of their descent from him, are ascribed rights in the agnatic corporation. In the event of the husband's death, then, rights over the widow revert to her agnates and rights over the children pass to his agnates. If the children are too small, separation takes place at a later time, when they are capable of being away from their mother's physical presence.

Finally, with respect to the rights that a man obtains over a woman through marriage, the usual anthropological terminology disguises the fact that it is not merely a question of *transference* of rights from the bride's father to her husband, but that marriage also *creates* new rights, namely those of sexual access, over the woman. Fornication and adultery are not distinguished by the Marri; sexual rights are created by the marriage ceremony where none before existed, and sexuality cannot legitimately be exercised outside the marital relationship. There are features of the marriage ceremony that may be interpreted as reflecting this fact (e.g., the adoration of the bride, cf. Appendix III). Otherwise, a woman's duties in her marital home are very much like her previous ones in her natal home, and one may speak of transference from father to husband of the rather comprehensive rights to demand submission and services.

With respect to bars on marriage, Islamic law seems to be accepted and largely followed. A man is allowed up to four wives simultaneously, while a woman may have only one husband. However, polygamy among the Marri is not very common even at the culmination of a male life cycle; its frequency in a gross census is roughly on the order of one household in twenty.

There is no kin-based exogamous group beyond the limits of incest, except for the rule, only recently accepted in the area, of unlawful conjunction—that is, a ban on having two near kinswomen, such as two sisters, as co-wives. With the addition of certain rules mentioned above favoring caste endogamy (pp. 30, 43), there are no further jural limitations on the permitted marriage combinations.

The transaction itself, however, is a reciprocal transaction in which rights over the woman are not only transferred from her father to her husband, and rights of sexual access generated, but also certain rights are obtained by the woman's father. The Marris distinguish two forms of marriage according to the nature of this counterprestation: either marriage with bride-price (*lab*) or woman-exchange marriage (*māttān*).

The bride-price is normally expressed by the Marris in terms of animals, forty, sixty, or eighty sheep, plus some cash, being given for a commoner's daughter. The verb used for such transactions is "to sell" the girl, and the bride-price is the subject of haggling. Important considerations here are the girl's attractiveness and status, but even more decisive is the degree of nearness between the groom and bride. "The bride-price [*lab*] on a second marriage, by a widow, is relatively the same—whether she is ugly, beautiful, old, young. But strangers [*seyyal*] always get much bride-price, and close kin [*wati*] very little." Sometimes the price is entirely dispensed with in marriages between agnatic cousins, especially where such marriages were, as often happens, a deathbed wish by one of the fathers. In exchange marriages, on the other hand, a small bride-price may be introduced when serious disparities in the age or beauty of the girls need to be counterbalanced.

When a bride-price is paid, the animals are taken from the herd of the household to which the groom belongs. This herd may be joint property of a group of agnates including the groom's brothers, father, and father's brother, and sometimes even agnatic cousins; but if any of them have separated out their animals in a distinct herd, they will give no contribution toward the bride-price. Likewise, an incoming bride-price goes to the herd of the household to which the girl belonged.

Obtaining a wife for a man is thus regarded as the responsibility of his father, which, in the event of the latter's death or if he shares an undivided herd with a senior agnate, devolves on another agnate in the position of head of the boy's household. The choice of means for obtaining a wife, that is, by bride-price or exchange, is in the hands of this senior agnate. The trend in the material is for a relatively high frequency of exchange as compared with bride-prices.

An interesting structural ambiguity results when certain persons may be at one and the same time within the contracting agnatic unit and favored as the reciprocal party to a marriage transaction. Take the case of two brothers with marriageable children. The senior of these brothers is the head, and it is his responsibility to provide the boys with wives, likewise to dispose of the girl in marriage. In a marriage transaction for his own son he may take a bride-price from the joint flock or use a girl, for example, his niece, in a marriage exchange. Finally, he may give his niece to his son in the favored FaBrCh alliance. In other words, for the groom the girl may be either a wife or a "sister" to be used in exchange to obtain a wife, according to the decision of his father as marriage guardian. Agnatic cousin marriages take place whether the herd has been divided or not, and there seems to be a tendency to dispense with bride-price, though an exchange is demanded if possible, even when the herd has been divided between the contracting brothers. If, however, the herd has been divided and the father of the girl in question is dead, then control by the surviving senior man over his niece is lost and marriage guardianship devolves clearly on *her* senior brother, who will insist on a strictly reciprocal transaction, with either bride-price or exchange.

The marriage transaction is further complicated by the fact that it has two main phases, betrothal (*sang*) and wedding (*nikah*), which may be separated by a long interval of time. The betrothal is the binding contract that creates an affinal bond. At that time the terms of the transaction are decided, and in the event of bride-price a part-payment is made. The closing of the contract is signaled by a rifle-shot, at which point the exchange, or the transfer of the part-payment, is regarded as completed. Should the affianced girl die before the wedding, the reciprocal exchange marriage must still be performed, and in the case of the bride-price the part that has been paid is kept by her household, though further payments are not claimed. If the affianced man dies, the exchange is similarly regarded as completed and her father is free to arrange any new marriage he sees fit, while any price paid at the first betrothal is kept by the girl's household.

The wedding involves a feast, given by the groom's household, in connection with the transfer of the bride from her natal to her marital home, and the payment of any outstanding part of the bride-price. On her wedding the bride also receives a small dowry (*daj*), usually of jewelry, from her own agnates. The two weddings in an exchange-marriage contract need not take place simultaneously or closely consecutively.

During the wedding ceremony a further status of "marriage brother" (*wakil-e-brath*) is created by the appointment of a man to speak on behalf of the bride. This is a quasi-kinship status comparable to godparenthood in many other cultures; it implies duties and responsibilities like those of a brother and the use of kinship terms. "I have a duty to watch over my marriage sister's welfare. If her husband is bad to her I must tell him not to beat my marriage sister. Why? Is she not my sister? My young son will address her as FaSi [*pupi*]."

The marriage brother seems by preference to be chosen among the men of the camp who are not the closest agnates of the bride. But, in spite of informants' insistence on its importance, it is a relationship to which reference is very rarely made in any later context, though the fact that Pehrson had served as marriage brother in one camp opened the way for me to assume the status, five years later, of classificatory MoBr.

Before betrothal, a woman is known as *nishtagan-zal* (literally, "sitting woman"), while, after the betrothal, she is considered and referred to as "N. N.'s wife," though the future spouses have no contact with each other until the wedding.

Betrothal may take place at any time in terms of the ages of the prospective bride and groom, not infrequently at an infant's naming day, which follows six days after birth. Occasionally—though this has been forbidden by the Marri tribal council—unborn children may also be promised in exchange marriages, on the gamble that they will be daughters. In general, the value of women for exchange marriages is less, the younger they are; so exchange marriages may be arranged for one mature woman now in return for a small girl and an infant —gambles which, if they come off, give a family two women for one in exchange. As for the wedding, a husband was traditionally permitted to demand his wife when she was only three or four years old, but by recent tribal council decision the parents can now refuse to give her to the husband until she has menstruated.

Residence after marriage is patrivirilocal; in the very few recorded cases of uxorilocal residence, there is a status differential in the husband's disfavor, while the advantages to him in residing with his affines are considerable.

Such property as may be held by the wife goes to her husband as her legal guardian, but many things she will lock away in her private box and refuse to hand over, while she retains a certain control over his management of the rest through the threat—which is frequently heard—that she will dispose of it as a gift to her brother.

A marriage may be dissolved at the will of the husband, but, if he can give no reasonable grounds, he supposedly can be made to pay a fine of Rs. 200 to the sardar, though "strong men don't do this." In this case the divorcing husband cannot retrieve any bride-price. If the woman runs away from her husband, she must go to the sardar or the local section leader and have him accept and confirm the dissolution of the marriage, whereupon she is given by him in a second marriage. Her divorced husband will then receive all or part of the second bride-price, though never more than the sum which he himself paid for her.

If a marriage is dissolved by the death of the woman, her belongings pass to her husband, who is responsible for the funeral and mourning ceremony. At the death of a husband, on the other hand, the widow reverts to her own agnates, but her dowry (*daj*) goes to her sons and sometimes also to her daughters; only if there are no children can she hope to be able to take her property with her. After forty days the widow may be remarried by her agnates. If she is old and has children who will look after her, she cannot be forced into a marriage by her guardian, but, unless she opts to remain unmarried in her children's home, all her connections with her former affines are severed, and her own agnates arrange her second marriage and receive her second bride-price without consulting or informing her dead husband's kin. Sayyids in the village settlement are an exception, in that they forbid the remarriage of widows.

There is a strong preference among the Marri for marriage between agnatic cousins, which expresses itself both in explicit statements of the ideal and in statistics on the relation between spouses, though it should be emphasized that this preference cannot be taken to be prescriptive—indeed, it is structurally impossible to make a prescriptive marriage system based on FaBrDa marriage.

"I have two sisters. They were both married to their own FaBrSos. When it came time for me to marry, there was no FaBrSo left for me so I married out of my own section. It is good to marry one's own; after all, one's own people are the best. Now I have three daughters and one son. We have made exchange with a FaBrSo, engaging my son to his daughter, and my daughter to his son. Now for Sasso [age three] there were no agnates left, so we engaged her to a Shirani, with bride-price."

As noted before, this marriage preference has a strongly involuting effect, which is also desired by the Marri. The leader of one camp asserted with satisfaction: "As close as the nail is to the flesh, so close are the men of our lineage to each other (*Nakon āš goržd nazikh e, čon ki kauma mardom nazikh e*)."

The kinship relationship of spouses in two different samples, one composed of tent camps and one constituting the village of Badra, both from 1955, are as shown in the accompanying tabulation. The total absence of non-Marris in

	FaBrDa	Other Agnate	Other Kin	Other Sub-section	Other Section	Non-Marri	Total
In tent camps	13 (30%)	14 (33%)	4 (9%)	5 (12%)	7 (16%)	0	43
In Badra village	26 (30%)	18 (21%)	10 (12%)	11 (13%)	1 (1%)	20 (23%)	86

the tent-camp sample is explained by the fact that more prominent leaders, among whom such marriages are mainly found, are almost all settled in villages. The 20 cases of non-Marris in Badra village may be broken down in the following subcategories: 9 reflecting political alliances, 5 with resident non-Marri clients, 3 with low-caste, and 3 with others.

The interpretation of some of the factors behind this pattern of choice will emerge in the subsequent discussion. Its implication in consolidating minimal lineages by counteracting the estrangement of agnatic cousins (cf. Barth 1955) was emphasized by Pehrson. An indirect implication, relevant to the discussion of kinship and reciprocity in the marriage transaction, is its effect in confounding any categorical distinctions between agnates, consanguines, and affines and between partners and parties to the marriage exchange. Not only do such categories fail to emerge as distinct collectives in transactions, but their abstract differentiation even becomes problematical when many persons occupy multiple and opposed positions. In several recorded cases in a relatively small sample, men have even married women of whom they are co-owners together with

Marri commoner—a major informant of the Pehrsons'.

other agnates of equal seniority—in which case they have had to specify bride-prices of which they then paid only a fraction, being themselves the recipients of the remaining fraction.

A description of a betrothal and a wedding ceremony is given in Appendix III illustrating and elaborating the character of the marriage contract, the parties to the transaction, and the nature of their relationship to each other.

The customary division of labor and authority between spouses strongly emphasizes the superordination of the husband. He should determine what shall be done, and when; he demands and controls. In the tent camps, the woman expects to grind flour, cook, and bake; fetch wood, water, and dwarf palm; plait, sew, and embroider; strike, pack, and pitch the tents; milk; and, to the extent the husband directs, do a share of the herding and harvesting. The men travel and trade, plow, seed, and do most of the reaping, threshing, and herding. The husband's ideal of a marital partner is revealed in the meditations of a leader, fearing that his sick wife might die:

"Where can I get another wife like her? I paid Rs. 4,000 for her. She does her work very well, she is young, she is beautiful. And when I get mad at her and beat her with my shoe, she doesn't get mad at me. She goes ahead and cooks good stew for me, good bread for me, then comes and takes hold of my beard and says 'By N. N. [their eldest son], don't be angry with me. Eat your bread, eat your stew. Forgive me.'"

The inequality is aggravated by the strict patrilocality and isolation of the woman from communication with her own kin.

"When I was married, I had not seen anyone of this house before, I had of course not seen my husband before. I was very lonesome and afraid and shy. For the first few months I said nothing to my husband and he said nothing to me. We slept together at night—that was all. For the first year, my heart did not want food. I ate little. All the day I said little. Often I cried. Now my husband and I have become older [about forty]. We have one son and one daughter, and seven dead children. Now we have become friends. But at first it was very difficult."

Without ruling out the importance of personal and altruistic attachments and loyalties, it is important to realize the tactical implications of the Marri marital relationship. The central question concerns what kind of accommodation it is feasible for the wife to try to make to a rather unrewarding situation. Jurally, the husband has all the rights and privileges—in the epigrammatic style of one female informant: "You know what rights a woman has among us Marris. She has the right to eat crap. That's all."

A woman in this structural position of subordination and isolation can hope to defend her interests by three main tactics: playing men off against each other, seeking alliance and support from other women, and minimizing contact with her husband. As will emerge in the next chapter, a mature woman can achieve much covert influence by playing her husband and her adult son off against each other or, in the case of agnatic marriage, by playing brothers off against husbands. An awareness of this power is implicit in comments cited on the advantages of agnatic cousin marriage and in the strategy of marriage described by an informant in Appendix III; it is also at the bottom of the objections sometimes made to exchange marriages: "The brother and sister will ally against the other brother and sister, and if one woman does bad work and the husband beats her, then that wife will tell her brother to beat his wife too."

The second tactic of alliance of women in support of each other is a characteristic feature of Marri life and combines readily with the third tactic mentioned, of minimizing contacts with the husband.

As mentioned previously, men and women engage in different economic activities, which separate them during the daytime; they are separated at mealtimes by bans on commensality; and they are segregated at feasts and at informal occasions alike. Further, Marri men see themselves as opposed by women, as fighting a continuous battle against female recalcitrance and laziness. Women even more markedly see themselves in a conspiracy of opposition against men, both for altruistic and opportunistic reasons:

"You know, it's all women's business, the giving or the stinginess, the helpfulness or the lack of helpfulness. What do the men know about the household affairs? They are away from home a lot, they sleep under a rock at noon, or under a tree, rarely in their tents. What do they know about what their women do?"

Yet rivalries between women prevent their wholehearted cooperation—rivalries between plural wives being most marked, but also rivalries between sisters and wives, wives and mistresses, etc., intrude and complicate conjugal and familial relationships.[1] In fact, the effects of these unstable and partly contradictory attempts by the women to adjust the imbalance of the conjugal relationship may be traced in most of the regular features of Marri domestic life. These crudely tactical considerations come particularly to the fore because of the very form they take—with minimization of contact between spouses and an accommodation based on lack of knowledge of the activities of the spouses, distrust and fear of discovery readily tend to widen the schism. The general cultural milieu is a further contributing factor—in their relations to superiors, to strangers, to almost anyone, Marris expect to be manipulated and cheated and tend to protect themselves by having only opportunistic transactions. A relatively harmless example of double deceit may serve as illustration. Women regularly remove wool

1. An illustration from Jean Pehrson's notes: "On migration today I saw a packsaddle that was half open, with an expensive copper pitcher and a brass bowl about to fall on the rock and break. I quickly ran to hold it together to prevent breakage, and asked the camp mistress whose load it was [to call the owner to fix it]. She said: "It's not mine, so just let it fall." [It belonged to her eldest son's un-favorite wife.]" However, see also a contrary informant's statement, p. 46.

from the household's stores when their husbands are away and there is an opportunity to exchange it for sugar and tea at a nearby caravan through the agency of young boys of the camp. Such supplies they keep hidden and use to make tea for themselves when the men are gone, to give their lovers, etc. When criticized for weighting her wool so disproportionately with dirt that she thereby compromised the opportunity of trade for the others, one old woman told her young helper just to cover the dirt as well as he could and tie it up, raising her eyes heavenward and exclaiming piously: "Oh God, only you can see [i.e., decide] my fate!"

In spite of such opportunities for accommodation, the pressure on the wife may be so extreme that it leads her to develop attitudes of intense opposition and hatred toward her husband. Thus the Pehrsons were approached by wives who wanted poison to kill their husbands, and the most extreme case, which also awed the Marris themselves, was the woman who put a curse (*svel*) on her own children in her hatred of her husband: "May the seeds of that man spread neither far nor last long in this world. They are unclean!"

The concept of uncleanness, of filth, is particularly relevant to the male attitude to the marital partner. Though the Marri folk version of the fall from grace is related to pollution and not directly to sex,[2] it is relevant in implying a close connection between the two:

"Adam and Hawa lived in a sort of Heaven, on the fruits that God gave them. When they ate, there was only a sweat that came from their skin, none of the uncleanness that we humans are contaminated by. But Satan meanwhile prayed to God to give him a place in people's hearts, and God granted his prayer. . . . So they went and ate the forbidden wheat. And when they had eaten, they felt the need to defecate. So in a lonely part of the Garden they defecated. When God came to see them the next morning he was very angry, saying 'Why have you polluted my holy Garden?' And so saying he took Adam and flung him toward the sun's rising, and Hawa toward the sun's setting."

However, the sexual act itself is also, in agreement with the Moslem view, regarded as polluting (*benamāš*). Likewise, a woman in her menstrual period is polluting; she does only the dirtier forms of menial work and she does not cook or bake, since no one would eat the food if she did. On the seventh day she washes and resumes her normal profane status. For forty days after childbirth, the mother is also polluting. In such periods, the husband does not sleep with his wife, though "of course, some men are fools, and go to their wives before the forty days have passed."

The woman in her marital role is thus particularly associated with pollution. This also finds expression in a (koranically sanctioned) disgust for pubic hair, which is carefully removed every two to four weeks. "If I died, it would

2. Though contrary to the account given in the Koran, this version seems to be widely known in the Moslem world.

be very bad for other people to see my hair, people would think I was awful. And if I didn't pick out my pubic hairs, my husband would fight with me." Men strongly express their disgust with their wives, and womankind in general—implying a dilemma which one old woman utilized in a taunt when she was being bawled out by her husband: "I suppose then that you men were not born of women, that you came pure from Heaven?"

Yet, by both men and women, sexual love is highly valued, and mutual desire between the sexes is taken for granted. In commenting on the adulterous activities of a mature woman married to an immature boy, people would not condemn her, since "if one is naked, one needs clothes. If one is hungry, one needs bread. If one is a woman, one needs a man."

The theme of love is most clearly expressed in love poetry, sung by both sexes:

"I saw a woman, lithe and graceful/like a high-bred Arabian mare./Her eyes, more black than coals/burned through my heart, and left their scars."

". . . my heart is with a flashing-eyed man/locked in the jail in Macch./I shall take myself to the Sardar/and weep and bare my head in supplication./He will give me the key to my lover's cell./Then will my heart be glad."

This relationship between lovers (*dostani*) is the central theme of Marri artistic expression and is the social relationship that is given far the highest value. A woman confiding in Jean Pehrson, when she heard rumors that her lover had tired of her, made the sociological comparison explicit:

"I have become such a fool over that man, so crazed by my passion for him, that even when they killed my own brother, I did not grieve. Even when my own son died, I couldn't grieve. My heart was with this Marri man. But now that this news has come I cannot eat, I cannot sleep, I often just for nothing burst into tears. It is very great, very hard, to be a lover for us Marris."

The outstanding structural feature of the love relationship is its categorical differentiation from the husband-wife relationship. The two are regarded as incompatible or even antithetical.

"Very few Marri women are lovers [*dost*] with their own husbands. It is not our way [*rānd*, literally: "footprint"]. Marri women have other men as lovers. And not just one here and one there, but everyone has a secret lover. . . . Those few Marri who are lovers with their husbands, they never let anyone see it, if other Marris are around they sit silently and say nothing to their husbands. It is a matter of shame to show anything."

In this polarity of marriage and love, and in the syndrome of adultery, hate, and passion that is associated with it, basic dilemmas of Marri culture come dramatically to a head.

As noted before, the punishment for adultery is death for both parties (by the hand of Hu, HuBr, HuFa and HuSo, HuFaBrSo, HuFaBr, woman's Br, Fa—in that order) or, alternatively, dishonorable divorce and remarriage. Secrecy and deception consequently being of primary importance, the systematic field material on which a discussion of the lover relationship may be based is necessarily limited and of variable nature. A prime consideration is also the need to distinguish different kinds of material and their relevance: the ideology as elaborated in poetry and myth, the rumors and accusations, the hinting and bragging, and the actual behavior as observed or confirmed beyond reasonable doubt by circumstantial evidence.[3]

Love as celebrated in poetry is romantic to the highest degree; it is frustrated by external circumstances; it is a fleeting bliss:

"Now my lover has come/He sits far away with other men./My husband forbids me to see him—/a curse on my husband, all of his days."

"Come once more to that hidden valley/gathering wood for your evening bread. /Come to me waiting in that valley/ere your camp moves to far grazing lands."

Besides the reciprocity of the love, several other aspects of the ideal relationship are constantly emphasized. Beauty is primarily important in the woman, but also in the man. Fearlessness is the man's most important virtue, whereas a woman is permitted to express her fear. Constancy is highly valued, as in the exchange:

"When I leave don't weep for me/My camp will be far away,/our homelands far apart./Do not miss me/do not trouble your heart./Find a new lover when I migrate /for our homelands are far apart."

"I shall grieve, my heart will break/for you, and for you alone./All other women are as dirt;/by my beard, I will love only you."

The same ideals find expression in the story of Mastantokri, the only Marri saint of any importance, and his mistress Sammo. Credited during their life with no acts that are meritorious by Islamic standards and with miraculous

3. The Pehrsons were very clear on these points in the field, and as a man-and-woman team they were able to make observations that no single fieldworker could match. Their most important data are from three camps, which they came to know very well, and which show a convincing dovetailing of the different kinds of material noted above and of these to other features of social organization. Of the basic facts of a high frequency of infidelity, accusations, and adultery killings there can be no doubt, as any person with intimate administrative experience with Baluchis can confirm; nor can there be doubt of the elaboration of these themes in love poetry. But for their detailed articulation in a social structure, these three camps—one in detail and two for supporting evidence—constitute the main material.

powers instrumental only in their love affair, their sole claim to sainthood seems to be the way in which they actualized the ideal love relationship.

"Mastantokri was a Powadhi shepherd who fell madly in love with a beautiful Marri woman named Sammo. She had beautiful red clothes, much jewelry and a pale complexion—a very beautiful woman she was. He saw her and became so foolish about her that he quit herding sheep for his master and instead herded her animals for nothing. She wove a tent for him and although her husband and others beat him and threw stones at him, he stayed. When her work was done at night he would call her to his tent for a meeting [majlis]. They would sit facing each other in the tent, and be together all night. When her baby would cry out in the next tent, Mastantokri would wave his arms in a swinging motion, and the baby's cradle would rock and the baby would fall asleep."

In actual life, the ideal of constancy is rarely adhered to, but, on the other hand, promiscuity is definitely condemned as incompatible with a lover relationship. Thus, when one woman bragged that three men had visited her the night before, when her husband was away, an older woman commented after her departure: "She just told us that to make us believe men think she is beautiful. Why—any woman's sex organ is beautiful—to men."

A second condition for the lover relationship is that it be completely voluntary—the seductive pleading and beseeching in the poems is matched in real life, and rape and prostitution are despised. The man should plead (minat kanagh) with the woman, and she must be won, by charm, because he is a good lover (shaunk-i-mard), and not by force. If other means can be kept secret, however, so that they do not interfere with the image of the virile seductor which the man seeks to project, they may be utilized. Thus love magic seems to be highly elaborated and frequently used.

"When someone becomes a fool [ganookh] about a woman, and she does not heed his pleas, he will go to a sorcerer [jahro] to get a charm, paying lots of money. The Gagdalis are the best, everyone down there understands witchcraft. If they aren't available, there are a few Marri sections that will do; one is Siahpadh [of the Sherani branch of Loharani]. Perhaps the charm will be salt, or thread, or dirt. The man will either sneak the charm himself into the woman's tent, often throwing it into the fire so that the smoke will carry the power to the woman, or he will give it to someone else to sneak there. The curse may take three directions: it may make the woman lust for the man, it may kill her, or it may make her ill, possessed by a jinn."

But if such secret means of affecting the woman are successful, they must be followed up by courting, to give the relationship the quality of romantic passion.

Gifts to the woman must be just that—they are tokens of love and must not be interpreted as payments. This is shown in the story of an unusually ideal love affair, where the lover is a nobleman and she his farm laborer's wife, thus diminishing somewhat the normal demand for secrecy (cf. p. 66):

"We came here when I was below puberty. N. N. followed me around for a long time asking for my favors. I refused because I was too young. . . . Then after a while we began seeing each other, I slipping away from my husband in the nights. Now for about eleven years he has had no other mistress nor I any other lovers. Most Marri women you know have first one and then another, but I was always true to him. He used to give me fine clothes, shoes, and saris, but now my husband won't let me accept gifts from him. You see my new palm sandals? Yesterday he brought these and said: 'If your husband would only let me I would bring you shoes of the finest leather. But all I can give you is palm sandals.' "

While meetings between lovers must of necessity be relatively few and brief, the reciprocal gifts can serve as private reminders of the relationship. The male's gifts are usually reciprocated by the woman with pieces of her own needlework, especially embroidered skullcaps and tobacco pouches—made at personal risk, since her husband would demand an explanation if he surprised her making them. Cryptic messages are also sent by way of close friends or kinsmen when they travel and visit camps—tiny silk-wrapped packages containing bits of cosmetics, pebbles ("my heart has become dry as a stone since I have not seen you"), etc.

The private, secret-lover relationship is to the Marri a thing of surpassing beauty and value. Through public suspicion and denunciation it becomes transformed into adultery (siah-kar, literally: "black work"), a dishonorable, shameful, and devastating thing. In the transition zone, when rumors circulate, when warnings are given, etc., the extent to which lovers live up to the romantic and chivalrous ideology is tested. The men in this situation, who also stand far the best chance of escaping death and dishonor in the event of discovery, very rarely reveal their fear; the only case recorded was of a man who was warned in private by an older kinswoman that his mistress' husband suspected, and exclaimed: "Oh FaBrWi, don't talk that way! It makes me sick to my stomach!" But women also can show great fearlessness, as one young wife when the camp shepherd warned her not to be so flagrant in her current affair:

"It's no concern of yours, it's my very own business. If I am foolish, it's only myself that will be hurt. You have your lovers and I have mine. If my Hu is going to do a certain piece of work [i.e., kill her], then it does not matter. If you want to eat your bread that I made and then go home and get your sword and kill me that's all right too. Now shut up."

In several cases there can be no doubt of the husband's suspicion, perhaps even knowledge, of the wife's infidelity. What precipitates action on his part is very difficult to specify. Informing by another man is also very dangerous, as the act in itself causes the damage to the husband's honor. It is public knowledge of the wife's infidelity, and not the infidelity in itself, that is damaging, and the husband may perfectly well strike at the informer rather than his wife. Intriguing women are probably more commonly the informers, though for them too there is danger, unless they themselves are without blame.

"No one has been killed for adultery in our camps [own, and FaBrSo's]. That's because we never tell. The other Marris are often killed for adultery—they tell tales. We say nothing. If I found out my BrWi was committing adultery, I wouldn't tell my Br. I wouldn't even tell on an unrelated [gharib] woman. This is all our women's business. We know everything, but we tell the men nothing."

On the other hand, sometimes it seems to take very little to precipitate an accusation, as in a tribal council case, according to the evidence of a woman found begging in Sindh four months after fleeing from her husband:

"One day I was carrying a small sack of grain on my head and an unknown man came along and gave it a push so that it fell off. Now my MoBr [who by tribal custom does not have the right to kill for adultery] was standing at the front of his tent and saw that. He said to me: 'Upon my beard, I will kill you and that man some day. You are surely black [i.e., an adulteress]. For what other reason would he have done that? By my beard, I will kill you.'"

An important factor affecting the probability of accusation is the status of the male lover. The risks run by a nobleman courting a commoner's wife are greatly reduced, as is the necessity for the husband to denounce the wife even in the case of common gossip. "They are leaders [mukadam]; they are worthy of respect [izat wali]. They can have a hundred mistresses and no one will kill them." On the other hand, caught in flagrante, they are in no way inviolable; thus in an escapade by a very prominent leader, as reported by his companion: "He didn't even finish last time, when he and I sneaked off together. N. N. [the mistress's husband] got up and filled his rifle and started out, but Mastantokri (the saint) made his eyes blind."

When a woman knows her husband has discovered her affair and plans to denounce her, she sometimes adopts the dramatic course of suicide. This would seem to constitute her final triumph over her husband—he is denied the possibility of defending his honor by killing her, while she dies unsullied, not as an adulteress but as a pure and perfect lover, in full defiance of her husband. In one camp of the group studied there had recently been such a case, and the woman was mentioned with great respect. She had hanged herself in her tent on realizing that she had been discovered, and the act of will needed to commit suicide by hanging from a tent apex 1.50 meters above the ground, with knees bent, until death has occurred deserves emphasis.

Action on the part of the wronged husband or his representatives should according to strict custom be preceded by a public accusation (*yahu*), naming the adulterous parties, but this seems in practice to mean very little, since a post hoc declaration that the matter concerned adultery is sufficient. The husband has the right to kill either or both adulterer and adulteress, or he can demand a divorce. In the former case, no blood revenge or compensation can be had for the killed man. In the latter case, the husband can claim at least a part of the bride-price obtained by his divorced wife's remarriage (cf. p. 43). Pending the remarriage, she lives in the home of the section leader, not with her parents. If after public accusation a husband does *not* kill or divorce his wife, the tribal council demands security money of him before the return of his wife, which he forfeits if he subsequently kills her. A woman once accused of adultery cannot again be accused—that is, in the event of divorce and subsequent remarriage, her new husband can never divorce her as an adulteress.

There are no records of the frequency of adultery accusations in a sample or among the Marri tribe as a whole, but their general prevalence as an important fraction of conflicts treated by tribal authorities is attested by tribal council members and local Pakistani representatives. Likewise, killing by all the categories of relatives who have the right to do so, including not infrequent killing of mothers by their sons, was attested. The situation in which the latter might happen was characterized by Marri commoners as follows: "If the man is lazy and incompetent, then for the sake of honor the man's son will kill his mother because she has become unclean [*gandagh*]."

As for the lover relationship, it appears to be universally taken part in by all married persons in the camps where really detailed information could be gathered. A song celebrating the virtuous woman was sung with irony and seems to corroborate rather than contradict this impression:

"I pass my days without the secret pleasures of my sisters,/without their secret fears I pass my days. /Why should I give my husband leave to kill me?/An early grave for fleeting bliss is a poor exchange. /I once before birth saw my mother's womb. /She after death is seeing my prudence."

Women, before marriage, however, do not take lovers, while boys do. With increasing age the frequency and intensity of the affairs decline. A woman just past menopause was embroidering a beautiful bag for eye-makeup (*surma*). "It is for a man who used to be my lover—he doesn't come around much lately, but we're still friends." The distribution of lovers, spatially and structurally, shows some characteristic trends. The pattern is typically one that connects persons in different camps as lovers. "We don't have lovers from our own camp men very much. Our own men aren't interesting to us. Once in a while a shameless woman will have a lover from her own camp, but that's very rare." This is a somewhat idealized picture, given by the informant against better knowledge; however, recorded cases were predominantly with non-camp members, and the disadvantages of affairs within the camp in terms of weakening the women's common front against the camp's men are obvious.

The kinship and tribal relations of known pairs of lovers may be tabulated as follows:

FaBrSoWi	2
Other close agnate's wife	1
Kin on Mo's side, other subsection	2
Unrelated, other subsection	10
Other sections of Marri tribe	6
Low-caste	3

The contrast between the distribution of lovers and the distribution of spouses is striking and reflects precisely the dispersal of the former over a wide range of camps with which ego's camp comes only intermittently into contact.

Within the camp there is evidence that adultery accusations, or threats of denunciation, can serve in a fashion analogous to witchcraft accusations in other cultures. The Pehrsons' servant, despised by the women of one camp for his refusal to be seduced, was shortly afterward accused of soliciting favors upon arrival in another camp. This accusation was connected with a general distaste for his presence there, and similar threats and insinuations seem to be used to rally camp opinion against unpopular shepherds attached to a camp, etc. Distrust and dislike of strangers is often expressed in terms of insinuations about their intentions toward the women of the camp. This suspicion not only readily adds itself to other characteristic Marri attitudes toward strangers but seems to stand as a convenient symbol and summation of them all.

The "explanation" of the syndrome of facts outlined above is problematical. Not only is there an inevitable paucity of data, but one is rather at a loss in evaluating available evidence and deciding on the relevance of data in the wilderness of secrecy, cheating, idealization, and self-deception surrounding these activities. Several factors that immediately spring to mind for an anthropologist seem never to be considered at all by the Marri. Thus, for example, the question of paternity in this fiercely agnatic ideology would seem to be crucial, yet it is never brought up by them. Take the case of a woman whose husband had seen her with a lover. He decided not to kill her, since she was eight months' pregnant and he wanted the child. But the man's brother conferred with their father, who said to kill her. So the HuBr hanged the woman from a tree with his turban, and "since then that tree does not change with the seasons, neither greens up in the spring nor drops leaves in the autumn, just stays the same as it was then." The issue as to whether the child might be the lover's is not raised—yet biological parenthood is recognized. The only situation in which the question of paternity seemed meaningful (or acceptable?) to informants concerned the status of children conceived by women while living in the section-leader's house pending a divorce. The expectation that such women were heavily in demand for sexual services was shared by all— but the question of legitimacy, it was claimed, would not come up in this case either, since the women would induce abortions, and no case could be found where a child had resulted. I can only suggest that the extraordinary contrast between having lovers and being an adulteress is connected precisely with this attitude. Two lovers have meetings, *majlis*, and there is a flimsy shred of ambiguity as to what takes place between lovers. After being told about the lover-saint Mastantokri and his beloved Sammo, the Pehrsons would sometimes ask the tactless question whether the two had intercourse when they met.

"In all their telling and all our asking, that question had evidently never occurred to anyone quizzed. Of those who would venture a guess, about half replied in the affirmative, giving as their reason 'they were lovers, weren't they?' The other half replied with an equally strong negative, reasoning 'since Mast was a saint, he must therefore not have done badness [*gandaghi;* here elliptical for sexual intercourse]' " [J. Pehrson, MS, pp. 53-54].

But an adulteress has dishonored her husband and his lineage, and as soon as she is "discovered in adultery" she is divorced or killed, so until she is declared an adulteress, her children must by definition be her husband's legitimate and genuine issue. There can, in this society, be no recognition of a distinction between *pater* and *genitor.*

By way of explaining these facts, I can thus do no more than restate their crucial features in summary form. The essential fact is the polarity of the lover and the marital relationships. In marriage, a man has comprehensive rights; the woman is his property, to use and dispose of, with very few limitations indeed. A minimum of interactions is voluntary on the part of the woman; inequality is maximal. The lover relationship, on the other hand, is one in which neither party has any rights—it is the only relationship in Marri culture in which men and women are jurally equal. Every interaction is voluntary; the male proves himself by being accepted, the woman by being wanted and by being an equal partner to the social transaction. The only other relationships experienced by a woman that partake of these qualities, though never to the same extent, are those with mother, siblings, and children. These—and secret lovers—are also the only persons who intimately eat together, out of the same food, in contrast to the absolute taboo forbidding the husband to touch food or water from which his wife has eaten or drunk. So also in the words of a lover denying rumors of faithlessness:

"Don't let those lies make a wound in your heart. You know how people are. Those with whom you eat bread, they may be your friends. But those whom you don't eat bread with, those people are sure to try to make trouble for you—tell black lies, thieve. You know how people are. Don't listen to them, my love."

The immense value attached to the relationship between lovers must derive from the fact that through it alone can adult men and women in Marri society establish a voluntary and mutually satisfying relationship.

The general argument in terms of which the material in this chapter has been presented might be summarized as follows: (1) Women in Marri society have no rights or responsibilities vested in them, and female sexuality is a source of pollution. Yet women are agnates and embody male honor. Men must protect themselves by controlling them through strict purdah until they are absolved from responsibility by transferring all rights to the husband. (2) Women are given, without rights, into marriage; yet they spring from honorable agnatic stock. It is dishonorable to give them to strangers, and it is good to keep them within the circle of close agnates. Political considerations, and the protection accruing to the women by these arrangements, further magnify the effects. (3) With a high frequency of agnatic cousin marriage, the parties to marriage transactions have no invariant correlates in a wider agnatic organization; the implications of marriage are structurally indeterminate. (4) Women have no rights vis-à-vis their husbands, and their sexuality is a potential source of dishonor. Husbands protect their interests by imposing strict purdah, while wives must protect their interests by non-jural means. (5) The non-jural means most readily available to wives are: forming a coalition with other women of the camp against the men and minimizing contact with the husband. Yet women are rivals for most goods, which they can obtain only through men: domestic organization and strife is significantly structured by fusion and fission among affinally related women. (6) A satisfying adult relationship between the sexes can be established notably outside the shackles of a Hu/Wi relationship of super- and subordination, that is, in a lover relationship. A whole syndrome of cultural traits is elaborated around romantic love and adultery, which come to have the greatest importance for members of the society.

The somewhat extreme lengths to which these features are carried can be understood in terms of the interrelations of most of the factors I have singled out in this analysis; they tend to connect in vicious circles with no apparent controls. The possible brakes on the system would seem to be fear and the community of interests that tends to develop between spouses through their participation and common pride in child-raising (cf. citation, p. 59). These controls will be further explored in the following chapter.

VI

THE CAMP COMMUNITY

"The wolf and the dog are brothers. They both said: 'The domesticated animals are mine!' Then they decided to divide them, but they were unsure as to the procedure. The dog suggested 'You go in that direction, I in this, and those animals that follow each of us will belong to the one whom they followed.' They departed in opposite directions and all the animals followed the dog. Now the dog will not permit the wolf to get at the animals, saying 'They followed me!' but the wolf says 'I have a share too!' and at night he tries to get some of the animals."

ENOUGH ANALYTIC aspects of Marri life have now been discussed for the central questions of community organization to be approached. A descriptive typology of the main forms of settlement was given in Chapter II. Most of the available material comes from one of these types, the free-moving tent camp, and some from the sedentary nucleus type, composed of many camps grouped around a small sedentary center. These tent camps constitute the traditional, and still today predominant, type of local group, and the following analysis will be concerned exclusively with them.

Before embarking on this analysis, one needs to establish as a fact that tent camps constitute significant units in Marri social organization. This cannot be taken for granted simply because they are physically discrete—indeed, as will be shown, this discreteness is rather more apparent than real. The fact that the scale of camps is considerably less than that embraced by the sphere of personal kinship, and that they do not constitute recognized segments in the formal political organization, might lead one to doubt their social discreteness and look for larger primary communities of some kind. The following analysis therefore first seeks to establish the status of the camp as the primary community among nomadic Marris by referring to the various conventions in communication and in the use of space that create and maintain social boundaries. Second, the organization of such camps will be considered with reference to the daily subsistence activities of the members and in respect to the forms of joint property and mutual obligation characteristic of Marri culture. By giving attention to the kinds of interpersonal relations that develop in camps on these bases, it becomes possible to identify the main fissive and aggregating factors that affect the size, membership, and history of Marri camps.

Marri camps are strikingly small, scattered, and superficially amorphous. They lack any standard shape or layout; they are variable in size and appearance and give no visible evidence of the sectional identity of members or the nature of the relations between them. Indeed, not only is the internal structure of the camps not indicated, but their very existence is frequently disguised: the tents are placed in low ravines, behind large boulders, or hidden among a scatter of trees, and the color of the palm mats blends with the buff of the landscape to make them even more inconspicuous. The contrast with Afghan Powindah camps is complete; those Afghan pastoralists, camping in the very same area, live in communities of from twenty to fifty large, black goat-hair tents, clustered according to the agnatic relations of the household heads and generally dominating the landscape from a low, open hillock, visible miles away.

The small scale and variability of Marri camps is implied by the standard term by which they are known: *halk*, which can also mean elementary family, tent household, or subsection of a camp. In the sense of a spatially separate, coresident, and jointly migrating unit, such groups tend to be composed of anywhere from one to eight or ten small households, usually about three or four. One or several of these households may, however, lack any kind of tent or shelter as visible evidence of their permanent existence as a unit. Furthermore, various degrees of jointness in ownership, production, and consumption, as well as the separation of the sexes for eating and even partly for cooking, make the separation into households somewhat ambiguous. Let us therefore initially look, not at the constituent parts, but at the camp as a whole.

Though a stranger approaching a Marri camp may have an impression of looseness and randomness in pattern, he is in fact approaching a living area that to the members of the camp is conceptually laid out and has clear structure. To an extreme degree, as compared with most other human communities, this structure is only in the mind of the participants; visible signals or modifications of the natural landscape are few or lacking, yet space for a variety of different activities has been allocated, and invisible barriers and divisions have been created. Most important is the barrier separating the community from the outside. Marri etiquette requires the approaching stranger to dismount at a distance of some hundred yards from the tents and proceed slowly on foot toward the settlement. This procedure makes it possible for some member of the camp to direct the visitor to the *otak*, or guest area, which is the only appropriate spatial point of contact between the camp and the outside world. The guest area need have no visible features at all, though often there are signs that it has been used before for sitting or sleeping. A general judgment of the possibilities afforded by the landscape, combined with a tendency to place the *otak* east of the camp, the way the tents face, may give the stranger an idea of what is the appropriate side from which to approach the camp and where the guest area will most probably be; but no public idioms exist for visually designating the *otak* area.

The arrival of visitors, by activating the characteristic Marri institution of the *hal*, also brings out other structural features of the camp. Whenever Marris meet, the formal greeting and information known as *hal* is exchanged; and in the case of groups, the spokesman of each group is its highest-ranking member. Thus, after an inevitable delay, the *halk-waja*, or leader of the camp (or, in his absence, the highest-ranking member present), will be the first to arrive at the *otak* area and initiate any formal interaction. Until then, boys or lower-status men may have brought mats or pillows for the guests, but no identification of the visitors or conversation containing information of any kind can take place until the time of the *hal*.

Besides conventional greetings, the *hal* contains a full announcement of the identity of persons, their purpose in traveling, and other items of news that may be of interest. The camp leader likewise identifies himself and the sectional position of the camp, as well as the main activities in which the personnel are engaged at the moment, and other local news. This done, subsequent interaction proceeds more freely and can be initiated by anyone present, based on the common understandings of structural positions that have been established.

The camp still retains large areas of anonymity and privacy. The identity of persons other than the camp leader need not have been divulged, whereas all the visitors should be introduced; the subdivisions of the camp and the identity of its women will certainly not be communicated. Each tent or living site remains surrounded by an area of privacy that must not be violated, and the well-bred visitor remains in the *otak* until he is invited and accompanied elsewhere. Usually the males of the camp will congregate in the evening around the male group's fire, generally that of the de facto most influential man, whether he be formal camp leader by seniority or not. The women, to a much less extent, sometimes form themselves in a female group around the fire of the *halk-waja's* wife, the *godi*. The men generally have a tree or a large rock, in the shade of which they congregate informally during the day, and frequently the camp leader has a chosen spot in a commanding position, from which he can direct activities when the flocks leave in the morning and return in the evening.

Not only are the internal barriers subdividing the camp there for the stranger; they are a continual feature of camp organization. Males will be hesitant to approach the women's fire, and each couple will jealously guard its area of private living space, resenting trespass near the tent. The limits of this private area are the limits of home. Children will have to ask their parents' permission (and will usually be refused) to sleep an occasional night with an age-mate and cousin, even though this may be in the open, in full view, a hundred yards from the paternal tent.

Within each area, space is allocated for different uses. On the edge of the private area there is generally an individual *otak* place for the male head of the family. Friends and kinsmen seeking him should go there, not to the tent. Close to it is the male fire, while the women's fire, over which also the bread is baked and most of the cooking done, is lighted closer to the tent. In the tent are piled the main belongings of the household: a sack of grain, the flour mill, a teapot and a few pots and pans, a thick woven cloth on which the bread dough is

Woman baking bread by her tent.

rolled out, and a griddle for baking; a small flat woven bag for salt; often one or more rugs or quilts, a clothes bag containing rags for patching, bits of embroidery and clothes in the making; a small tin box locked with a great padlock in which the tent mistress' most valuable possessions are kept: a comb, needles, embroidery thread, amulets, herbs for medicinal and cosmetic use, and small quantities of tea, sugar, spices, and sweets. There is usually a sheepskin bag or two for churning and for storing clarified butter, and, at the side of the tent on a bed of rocks, the goatskin bags for water. Finally, there are ropes of twisted dwarf palm for securing these belongings on the load animals; there are rope-net packsaddles and a number of plaited mats for protection against the sun overhead during the day and the stones beneath at night.

Outside the tent, close enough so the property can be guarded, is the place for sleeping at night, while farther away a suitable area is set aside for a corral for sheep and goats and for the cattle. The shepherds generally drag their mats out to sleep in the midst of their flocks, to protect them against wolves and thieves. Even at relatively impermanent camp sites, the memory of these spatial arrangements remains. Thus people regarded it as important to show me, five years later, the exact location of the Pehrsons' tent and *otak*, at sites where they had spent only two or three weeks and to point out the three rocks over which the griddle for frying bread had been laid and the place where the waterskins had been stored.

Only on the basis of intimate knowledge of the personnel and interrelations of a camp can some degree of regularity and meaning be found in spatial distributions. There is a tendency for tents to align in an arc up against a hillock, enclosing a corral area for the better protection of the herd against thieves and predators at night. The tent of the dominant male in an integrated camp, then, tends to be in the center of such an arc or centrally located in any other configuration that the camp may have, while the tents of contenders to camp leadership tend to be as far separated from each other as possible.

In contrast to this lack of standardized visual expression of formal structure, certain features of verbal usage are highly stereotyped. The material here is merely impressionistic, yet some very striking patterns can be noted. Besides ordinary conversation, at least three forms of speech can be distinguished: the *hal*, commands, and poetry and ballads. These differ greatly in their subject and the kind of statements one is permitted to make in them, as well as in their formal style.

The *hal* greeting is spoken in a very low voice and in a continuous murmur through each sentence, rising in pitch at the end. It is unaccompanied by expressive movement; it is limited in content by formal "tea-party" rules of politeness. "Of course, you never mention any news that is really important." Juicy scandal or personal judgments are banned from it; they come out later, if at all, in the *majlis*—the informal bull session of the men.

Commands, orders, and instructions, on the other hand, are loud, as they often need to be shouted. They are prefaced by a long "Oooooo" cry and said in a high, level pitch and with continous volume, without pauses between sentences. This style can be assumed only by superordinate to subordinate; it expresses authority and need not be supported by imperatives and invectives, as does the exercise of authority through ordinary speech.

Poetry is restricted as to place and occasion; several distinct varieties of it can also be distinguished. Heroic ballads recounting the traditions of the tribe or section, or the exploits of semilegendary figures like Mir Chakur, are sung around the men's fire. These ballads are presented with excessively rhythmic diction, quickly and with a continuous flow of sound, trailing at the end of each song. Often they are accompanied by the shepherd's pipe (*nar*), involving a joint performance by singer and musician. Honorable men are hesitant to sing and will not play the flute when many strangers are present.

Love songs, on the other hand, are much more complex rhythmically and melodically and would be sung only by the men's fire by a member of the despised caste (Lori or Domb) who serve as quasi-professional musicians (*nari*). Such songs are most often sung by women while away from the camp, and then only when in small groups. They may not be sung by women in camp, and even lullabies (*lolis*) should not be sung in the presence of men. It is difficult to judge the place of love songs in the meeting of lovers; in semipublic they serve as a vehicle for the expression of facts and values banned from all ordinary conversation. Thus persons who in ordinary speech categorically deny the possibility of adultery in their section can proceed to sing a seductive love song and give moving expression to its romantic themes.

In everyday life, finally, talk in the camp, particularly between women, is often very liberally interspersed with swearing, largely of an obscene nature.[1] It would seem reasonable to assume that this usage serves to mark off yet one more distinct form of speech and meaning.

We can thus isolate a basic framework for all social interaction that takes place in a camp: it is structured by a compartmentalization of space by allocation for various uses and degrees of privacy and exclusiveness, and it is segmented by a typology of forms of speech with accompanying restrictions on topics and occasions for which their use is appropriate.

Other regularities in the activities of camp members relate to the practical and material necessities of life. In the daily round of activities in a camp, we can recognize a number of tasks that are essential, in the sense that unless they or their functional equivalents are performed, the camp cannot long persist, physically or economically. The particular form and organization of these tasks, however, are idiosyncratic of Marri culture. This combination of imperative problems and stereotyped solutions imposes a number of common characteristics on life in all Marri encampments.

First, in order to persist at all, the members of the camp must be able to agree on a joint migration policy. Since they are nomadic, persistence as a group requires continual positive agreement about moving and camping, which means in effect that each camp will be relatively homogeneous with respect to wealth and subsistence pattern, for the following reason: Marri nomadism is of mixed

---

1. "By my father's bad smell." "I'll squeeze out your crap." "May God make you polluted." "May your bones turn to ash." "You black wild animal [pig]." Woman to nephew, asking for water: "Can't you see my hands are busy. Do you want me to piss in your face?"

character, relating to herding, agriculture, and migrant labor, as described in Chapter II. Each of these activities has its own cycle and its own optimal pattern of movement. They can be, and generally are, combined, but will then exert partly conflicting pulls on those participating. Any migration policy will be a compromise between these different pulls and thus assumes a certain configuration of capital and labor resources. Only households with roughly equivalent assets and structure will be satisfied with the same migration policy, so only such households are able to stay together in a community through the year. However, the possible routes are many and the relevant information is incom-

Nomad camp with thorn enclosure for the herd.

plete; thus, even within relatively homogeneous camps, agreement about migration is difficult to attain and always remains a dominant issue. This issue will be discussed further below in connection with camp leadership.

Actual joint tasks, on the other hand, are few. The men of the camp will combine for a few special occasions, such as sheep-dipping, search for lost animals, or defense of the camp; otherwise they work singly or, at most, in pairs.

Women more frequently work in groups of two or more, as on their expeditions to fetch wood, water, or dwarf palm. In such tasks, little if any cooperation is involved in the actual tasks themselves, but there is evidence that it is considered necessary to help safeguard a woman's reputation, and it gives women an opportunity for gossip or singing, free from surveillance either by males or by husband's mother or sisters. Women also form teams of mutual assistance, as in making quilts or embroidering a new bride's dress. When plaiting dwarf palm, working in teams allows them to complete large mats while the palm fronds are still fresh and pliable. Such female work groups are ad hoc and rarely contain a full complement of the women in a camp, and there is much petty factionalism and complaint about not being asked to join, not being helped, or being let down on fair reciprocity.

The daily rhythm of the camps is dominated by the needs of the animals, except in those few camps that are essentially without stock. With the variety of animals that the Marri keep, and the techniques of management and tending that they use, a great deal of labor is tied up in herding. Thus in a large and only moderately wealthy camp of forty-three persons all told, eight persons were necessary for shepherding, even on festival days and weddings. In a smaller, wealthier camp, four out of twelve persons were full-time shepherds. These shepherds are mainly males: young adults and old men for the main flocks and teen-agers or children, sometimes girls, for the lambs and kids. They are away from camp from early morning until shortly before sunset, dispersed over a large area, leaving the camp depleted of male members during the day.

In addition, men do the plowing and most of the agricultural work; this work is generally located in areas unsuited for grazing and thus often at a great distance from the camp. Periodically, therefore, one or two adult males of the camp will be absent for one or several weeks, living in a small shelter by the fields and doing the required labor there. They are often accompanied by a wife, sister, or brother's wife, who cooks and washes for them.

Other men are also frequently away for one or several days, buying and trading, fetching grain or equipment from stores, scouting for pastures and water, hunting, or attending to political matters or legal claims before a chief or a council. Periodically, the camp may thus even be left entirely without males for a time.

The women are also repeatedly drawn away from camp, albeit within a somewhat closer perimeter. They must fetch water, often at several miles' distance from the camp, and search the hills for wood for their fires. There is a constant need for fresh dwarf-palm fronds, which are used for sandals, ropes, and mats and which are collected from various favored sites with a view to their higher quality. Finally, collecting wild onions, roots, and fruits adds both relish and substance to the diet.

The result of these patterns of work and movement is the continual dispersal of personnel. Not only are the locations of camps variable and unpredictable, but the presence of any particular person in his camp is less than probable, and his whereabouts at any particular moment, especially during the day, is unpredictable. Indeed, camps do not represent the concentrations of personnel that one might imagine; they are the (movable) points of reference but not necessarily of localization of people. The population is at every moment spread thinly and widely over the landscape. Even in the most desolate and uninhabited corner, one meets people—men traveling, boys herding, women collecting dwarf palm. The permanence and continuity of camps must be founded on the continual commitment of persons to them, not in their simple location in them. The specific form of these commitments will also serve as constraints on membership, in terms of which the social composition of camps may be analyzed.

This commitment of persons to their camp seems in the main to involve the Marri concept of *sharikh* ("jointness" or "sharing"). It covers the various degrees of joint ownership in herds and agricultural produce, it may be used to indicate a joint economy as a household or an extended household, or it may refer to the joint obligations within a camp for the expenses of hospitality. Even the fiercely defended private property in a housewife's locked tin box is in part subject to these claims by others—hence the lock and the attempt on her part to keep its contents secret.

The most important level of jointness is that of the joint herd, involving simultaneously a joint or coordinated labor pool for shepherding and agricultural work. It thus implies a share in an undivided estate of considerable value and membership in a functionally differentiated cooperative productive unit.

It is in the nature of the case that such a group must also share the profits from the herd and the fields and, to that extent, constitute a single extended household. However, the joint owners of a herd will rarely live in a single tent, or cook jointly, or eat jointly. Normally each married woman has her own stores and budgets and cooks for her own, independent domestic unit. The most clearly defined cooking unit is that associated with bread: each elementary household uses its own hand mill and its own iron-bound soapstone griddle for baking bread, while other foods may be prepared individually. The only interruptions in the regularity of bread-baking are caused by the housewife's menstrual periods, when a daughter, or another woman in a clean state, substitutes for her. The actual commensal unit is even smaller for everyday purposes; each adult male eats separately, or with unmarried sons, of the food which his wife has cooked or which he has prepared for himself. At festive occasions, on the other hand, men cooperate in cooking and eat in large commensal units; women also may form a similar, separate unit.

Because of this segmentation of the joint herd-owning group, the nature of the jointness within it becomes a matter of much variation and also of suspicion and recrimination:

"*Sharikh* means owning property jointly. The last time my younger married son returned from the bazaar, he opened his packages in my tent, showed me his tea and sugar and gave me half of each. That is real *sharikh*. All that *sharikh* means with my older son's sugar is that if I went to his wife and asked for sugar, she would be obliged to give me a share."

At the same time, obligations are also shared by more inclusive groups than those owning joint herds, and these obligations are of a kind that limit the autonomy of owners in their husbandry decisions. Thus the camp as a whole shares the expenses of hospitality and also the accruing reputation and honor. When guests arrive who must be honored by the slaughter of animals, each herd-owning unit provides one animal in turn, so as to distribute justly the economic burdens involved in the camp's external relations.

Finally, the obligation of hospitality itself springs from the widest and most comprehensive application of the idea of sharing: that rights to food cannot be preempted by any order of group, that food is God's bounty and should be shared freely by all. This ideal of universal rights of access to food, though strongly held, is never fully realized. "When someone slaughters an animal, and I hear about it or see it and they do not give me any, I get very sick. My bones ache and this shoulder in particular aches. If they give me just a small piece of the meat, then I am all right. . . . Many other women have this same complaint."

There are social controls to prevent the misuse of the hospitality obligation, and the strength of the obligation and the quality of the hospitality offered are proportional to the rank of the visitor. Nonetheless, even this widest of obligations is felt strongly enough so that women who do not wish to share feel obliged to hide food when they see strangers approaching, and it is quite inconceivable that anyone should ever eat or drink in sight of others without offering them a share.

The various degrees of jointness through the community might then be diagrammed as in Figure 8.

Such a pattern of joint rights can be maintained only if there is an accepted, institutionalized procedure for joint decision-making on policy choices and for the allocation of the burdens and rewards of jointness within the group. To analyze Marri camp and domestic organization, one must understand these procedures and the nature of their actual operation and effectiveness. It is made all the more difficult because of the evident and profound lack of trust and confidence that characterizes Marri attitudes even to their closest kin and that would seem to militate against any kind of enduring relations of jointness.

The most pressing recurrent issue is that of allocating the rewards and burdens of joint enterprise fairly between the constituent cooperating units, down to the level of individual shares—a matter that concerns Marris profoundly, and around which there is a concentration of attention and cultural elaboration. The dominant notion seems to be a principle of balance, that no person or group can be asked to contribute more than he will profit, coupled with an expectation that every participant in a joint venture will pursue his own self-interest to the bitter end. The result is an insistence on safeguards and an elaboration of techniques of just sharing as a prerequisite of any kind of relation of jointness. When that is technically impossible, each subunit should have an equal chance to lose or gain, by as perfect as possible randomization and, preferably, by a procedure that corrects for chance inequalities over time. Between unequals, on the other hand, high rank gives privilege but also implies expense. Always, the allocation procedure that makes the least use of human agents for decision-making is regarded as the most just, since all persons are expected to be partisan and opportunistic.

Because only few camps are built around a central person of unequivocally higher rank, the principle governing sharing between equals is the one that has

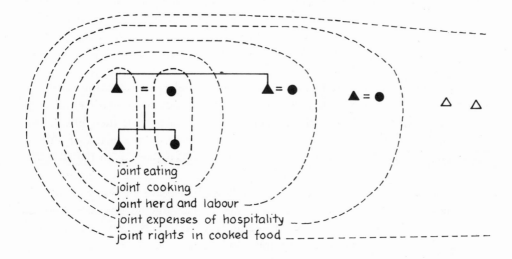

joint eating
joint cooking
joint herd and labour
joint expenses of hospitality
joint rights in cooked food

FIGURE 8

relevance in most tent camps. Within such a camp, the sharing may take place between three orders of subunits: between herd-owning units (*halk*), between tent households centered on a bread-baking fire (*loghansari:* "per fire"), or between persons—either males (*mardansari:* "per male"; *kairmiz:* "straight as male urine") or all individuals (*mardoomsari:* "per man," "per person"). In the last case, the precedent of koranic inheritance may be invoked to give male children twice the share of female children.

As between such parties, several techniques of randomization are used, employing goat pellets or twigs. For a for-or-against decision, goat pellets—one marked for, one against, and three unmarked—are shaken in the hand and dropped out one by one, the first marked one to appear deciding the issue. To decide whose turn it is to slaughter a sheep for hospitality, each contestant marks a goat pellet, the contestant whose mark comes last losing. In this case, either he may be made to kill his animal without compensation, but be excused from participating in the subsequent lotteries until all have slaughtered in turn, or else he may be given compensation; for example, of A, B, C, and D, D's pellet comes last, so he slaughters, but the others each give him 5 rupees (since 1 lamb = 20 rupees' value).

In dividing the animals in a joint herd, or the increase of a flock between owner and shepherd, twigs are generally used. The herd is divided into small groups of three or four animals of equal value in terms of age, sex, and condition. The contestants mark or choose twigs, and a person uninformed of their choice throws a twig on the back of an animal in each group.

The same procedure is used for dividing the meat of a feast: roughly equal shares are made, and contestants choose twigs, which an uninformed person places on the different helpings. Alternatively, goat pellets may be marked, the person whose pellet drops out first having first choice, etc. If a high-ranking visitor is present at the feast, he receives more and better meat, taking his share (niami-wand: "the middle share") first.

Such techniques are used only to solve the problem of allocating goods or social obligations justly. They do not seem to be associated with any mystic ideas of luck or divine will; the expectation seems to be that their effect, over time, will be random and equal. Nor are they used in the place of rational decision-making.[2] Thus, where policy decisions are necessary, as in the allocation of tasks to the members of a labor pool or in the determination of migration routes, entirely different procedures are followed: decisive authority is formally ascribed and exercised. Thus it is the camp leader and no one else who can announce the decision as to where the camp will migrate. But such an announcement may be the result of a very long and intricate decision-making process: one or more camp members may have to scout the area and collect further information; persons with various interests try to exert pressure, directly or through intermediaries; there are meetings and arguments, and subgroups separate out to arrange internal agreements and plan the tactics of negotiation, where several camps are involved. The women of the camp also voice their opinions, as when one camp was driven out of a territory by Pathans: "May the Marris and the Pathans get lost, with their interminable fighting. I am dying to sit in one place. But if we have to move, why are we going to Chamalang, where there are more Pathans? Why not go three migrations farther to our own Marris?" As the ones who do most of the labor involved in packing and

2. In some situations these same techniques are used for divination and thus affect decision-making when information is inadequate. Thus, to divine whether an engagement is impending and whether it, or some similar project, will be blessed, women take five goat pellets, marking one for the devil (Shaitan) and one for the good-luck angel (Mistagir), and drop them out of a closed hand one by one. If the devil's mark comes first, the engagement will be far away/ the project will be unlucky; if the good-luck angel's mark comes first, then it is close/lucky. If the three unmarked pellets come first, then it is Allah's pleasure (tir) as to what will happen.

moving, women are in a position to sabotage moves and to cause trouble in a variety of ways, so they also are listened to and their opinion is given weight. But most important are the opinions of independent herd-owners, who can threaten to defect from the camp if a contrary decision is pressed too hard. Such threats can readily be effectuated, since most persons have close kinsmen who will receive them and help them in other camps, and most cases of camp fission or restructuring seem to be immediately caused by such disagreements.

Nonetheless, on the formal level the position of authority is clear and explicit and is ascribed to adult males by lineal and collateral seniority. Thus, father holds authority over sons, senior brother over junior brothers. But the justification for taking ability into account is also recognized, and the two formal principles of seniority can come into conflict even in the relation between agnatic uncle and nephew, that is, between the senior son of a deceased senior brother in a sibling group and a surviving junior brother. Deep and fierce rivalries readily develop between such pretenders to formal leadership, generating destructive stresses in the joint group for which they are contending.

Thus, the set of commitments that connect persons to their domestic group, herd-owning group, and camp may be important but are also deeply ambivalent. The need for elaborate precautions to defend one's own interests in these intimate groups, even in the context of sharing the meat of a feast, the distrust of leaders, and at the same time the competition for leadership according to conflicting principles of ascription, all seem to militate against any enduring kind of jointness and rather to foster continual divisive pressures on every order of group. Moreover, fission is always a possible course: among the Marri, a man can terminate any kind of cooperative relationship in which he finds himself. When the relationship is contractual, the terms of its abrogation are contained in the conventional contract itself. But also when cooperation derives from a kinship relation, like that between father and sons, the economic aspect of the relationship can be discontinued by an institutionalized pattern of division and separation.

This separation is made by a division of the productive capital necessary for subsistence and, if desired, a subsequent parting of the ways. A son obtains, as his birthright, access to all pastures in the Marri area and a share in the joint land of his lineage; for these he is not dependent on the agency of his father. Beyond them, he needs animals for a herd and can demand a share from his father's herd. In such divisions a father retains twice the share given to each son, and all sons share equally. Thus a man with two sons will give each son one-fourth of the herd, keeping half for himself; one with four sons will give one-sixth to each son, retaining one-third as his own share. Several informants, among them young married men who had opted for a division, were under the impression that sons who had separated out had no further rights in the father's estate, which would then eventually go to the sons who remained with their father. By custom law, however, a son still has a right to share in the father's part of the herd when the father dies, even if some of his brothers have continued in an undivided estate with the father.

There are thus essentially no bars to the dissolution of the commitments of jointness that tie men together in herd-owning units and camps, and there would seem to be strong pressures conducive to fission, which raises the naïve question why Marris live in communities at all. Indeed, some can hardly be said to do so; one does find single tents, encapsulated in their suspicion and distrust of all others, maintaining themselves as individual units in relative isolation from all outside contact. In a certain sense, as shown in the discussion of the dispersal of personnel in the pursuit of subsistence (pp. 78 f.), this withdrawal might even be regarded as an ecologically optimal pattern in the harsh and barren Marri environment.

However, just as there are pressures driving people apart, there are also forces drawing them together. If there are psychological needs for a "we-group" and limits to man's tolerance of isolation from the society of his fellows, one might seek the community-building factors there. In the case of Marri tent camps, however, there are more purely sociological and more demonstrable factors at work, notably the personnel requirements of Marri subsistence and the needs of security and defense.

The pattern of Marri subsistence, and the needs for a variegated labor pool which it implies, have been discussed above (pp. 5-11): herding, agriculture, and migration make simultaneous demands that can be satisfied only by co-operation between several men. This need is a compelling force for the formation of larger communities, as is demonstrated by the prevalence of shepherd contracts. Marris express a clear distaste for having strangers close to them—yet, when the need for labor cannot be satisfied within the domestic group, they feel compelled to encourage and pay such strangers to join an understaffed camp. This arrangement is regarded as far from ideal, and difficulties of all kinds are anticipated. "I usually give a shepherd three chances—on theft, lying, etc., and then send him away. For adultery, however, he goes immediately." Nonetheless, the need is great enough for shepherding contracts to be frequent— that is, the tie of mutual need for cooperation is sufficient by itself to create a community of several domestic units among Marri pastoralists.

A straight shepherding contract with an entirely unrelated man, is however, a last resort. Lacking unmarried men and boys within the domestic unit, one turns, first, to poorer agnatic collaterals and to matrilateral and affinal relatives. Second, one prefers a *botar* ("animal owner"), who will herd his own and his employer's animals jointly, to a plain *pahnwal*, a man whose whole income is from shepherd's wages. Thus, of the thirty shepherds in five camps, fourteen were immature sons of herd-owners, eight were mature agnatic collaterals, and three were unrelated. Only two or three of the last two categories seem to have been without animals of their own.

Fear of animal theft, as well as suspicion of adulterous intent, clearly serves on the camp level to keep camps separate and to create a need for more personnel within the camp so that men will be available at all times to protect the women and the animals. Furthermore, there is a need for strength in numbers to provide basic security and defense of property and life in general. All such considerations can be grouped together as a second factor leading to the union of several domestic units in a community. That such a factor is operative is perhaps most clearly demonstrated by a comparison of the size of camps under different conditions of external threat. The camps using pastures within the Marri tribal area are more secure than those beyond the Marri boundary to the north living as strangers on the lands of Pathan tribes. Though not documented systematically, the difference in size between camps in these two areas is apparent: in the Marri area, with the greater security of being on their own lands and within the jurisdiction of their own tribal authorities, camps are small, rarely exceeding four domestic units, even among wealthy herd-owners. Pehrson, looking for camps sufficiently large to make prolonged residence profitable, found them only among the camps moving in Pathan territory, where groups of six, eight, and even ten households occur.

The fact that more tents band together in response to the greater dangers of living in a more hostile environment is also indicated by other evidence. During some weeks of tension in Marri-Pathan relations a second large Marri camp migrated and encamped close to the group with which the Pehrsons stayed, causing confusion during migrations and heavy pressure on available pasturage and water supplies; they persisted in this despite being taunted for seeking security by "living in Bob Khan's shadow." In that same period, which culminated in some days of skirmishing and forced migrations, great concern was expressed for members of the camp who were absent doing plowing, and the camp migrated *en bloc* rather than dispersed and individually as under normal circumstances.

Thus, although the daily activities and dilemmas of living together produce fissive conflicts within tent communities, there are also some compelling forces that aggregate persons in units of common or complementary interests, and the forms of Marri camps under various local circumstances may be understood as the result of their counterbalancing effects.

VII

THE COMPOSITION OF CAMPS

THE DESCRIPTIVE treatment of camps in the preceding chapter led to the isolation of certain factors as determinants of camp size and membership. In view of the complexity of the factors involved, and their possibly diverse and contradictory effects, a closer and more stringent analysis is needed of the connections and explanations I have posited. In analyzing the social organization of camps, I shall concentrate on their composition in terms of the reciprocal statuses of coresident members and on the processes of recruitment whereby camps persist or change their patterns of membership through time. It is in the nature of our concept of status that such an analysis will depict the main regular features of the interrelations of members—in other words, the main organizational features of the camps.

In the last part of the preceding chapter we isolated two major factors that lead to the aggregation of persons in camps. These factors have the advantage that their effects can be demonstrated against the external variables of demography and security; one can thus argue that they not merely are a way of summarizing empirical observations of camp form but are determinants of this form. Though they do not explain the particular social composition of camps, they may be expected to act selectively on different possible forms of recruitment and thus have certain effects on this composition. Likewise, the various fissive pressures I have described are also determinants of camp composition to the extent that they act differentially on social partners according to the specific relations between those partners. By a reformulation of this whole set of factors, it should be possible, if they have been correctly identified, to construct a model that depicts the determinants of Marri camp form and thus will generate the observed varieties of Marri camp composition.

Since other approaches to the analysis of community composition are characteristic of the anthropological literature, some justification of the present procedure may be called for. The alternatives may perhaps be characterized as the "idealist" and the typological approach.

An "idealist" analysis of Marri camp composition could take as its point of departure the explicit Marri value that a camp should be coterminous with the men of the *waris*, or minimal lineage, and their wives. Indeed, charts of composition (Charts I-III below) show a strong tendency in this direction. The ideal composition, however, is never realized—some or many close agnates in the *waris* are missing, while non-agnates are usually present. Thus, no camp will correspond to this ideal, and every camp must be described in terms of its deviation from the ideal. More importantly, the implications of such an approach are unclear. The claim that the ideal of lineage segment coresidence is the efficient cause of the preponderance of agnates in camp is both doubtful and incapable of demonstration. Unless this claim is implied, however, the fact that such an ideal is expressed by the Marris is hardly relevant, and nothing has been achieved by the approach other than the summary of the set of charts of composition by an inappropriate oversimplification.

Alternatively, a typological approach would take as its point of departure the actual charts of composition and devise a classification for them in terms of certain common empirical characteristics. With the present material such an approach is made difficult both by the small number of fully documented camps and by their bewildering variety of forms. Besides, such an ordering of the material does not bring us very far on the way to understanding the constraints that produce the typological patterns. For their discovery one still needs to turn to the type of material explored above: the culturally recognized forms that jointness and separation may take among the Marri and the factors that influence persons to establish or to discontinue an association with each other.

I therefore chose an approach using a generative model in this analysis of Marri camp. The analytic status of such a model is somewhat analogous to that of the componential model utilized in the analysis of kinship. In the following pages I shall simply try to explore, with some rigor, the cumulative, combined effects of the various factors I have isolated, to see whether they will in fact generate the features of camp composition that Pehrson recorded and that we seek to understand. Such exploration is most simply done in a stepwise fashion, introducing one factor at a time and examining its implications. Subsequent factors will progressively modify the picture produced by the previous factors alone; by the end of this deployment, one should have a fairly sound and complete picture of the forms of local groups that will be generated by the combination of factors that make up the model.

In other words, we shall now embark on a logical exercise, with concern not as to whether the statements we make are true of empirical Marri society but only as to whether they follow from the model at a certain stage of deployment. Only the end result of this discussion, that is, the form that *all* the factors in combination generate, is expected to correspond to empirical features of Marri camps, and the degree of fit between the two will be the measure of the adequacy of the model. But, since at this stage it seems impossible to make any model of a social system sufficiently rigorous, we shall have to assume, throughout, the general context of Marri culture as described so far and thus make occasional appeal to empirical facts to guide our deductions. When this generative exercise is completed, a fairly detailed account of the structure and development of one camp will be presented so that the adequacy of the analysis can be judged.

Initially, let us start with a population of isolated married couples. One basic factor in the formation of larger groups of coresidents will be natural increase; all new persons are born into households from which they receive their initial position in society and within which they exercise joint rights with other members. However, because Marri men, with their concept of male dominance and honor, insist on virilocality at marriage, only the birth of sons will have the long-term effect of causing an increase of numbers in such isolated units.

This factor of natural increase combined with virilocality will continually affect the composition of the Marri camp. Alone, it would lead to the development of camps composed solely of the men of a single descent group, and their wives and unmarried daughters, in ever-increasing numbers; such camps would also constitute single herd-owning units.

As noted, however, we need also to consider various factors that lead to the fission of camps. The factors emphasized in the discussion above are (i) difficulties over sharing, (ii) conflicting interests and judgments regarding common policy, particularly migration, (iii) fear, suspicion, and the discovery of adultery, and (iv) competition for formal leadership in camps. Each of these factors, singly or in combination, may cause a group to divide. Unless their occurrence is positively correlated with collateral distance *and* antagonists mobilize support strictly according to an agnatic descent charter, their effect will be to reduce the degree of correspondence between camp and descent group.

(i) Difficulties over sharing arise mainly within joint herd-owning groups, since the occasions for them are much more frequent within such extended households than between them. One may assume their effects over time to be cumulative, leading through decreased trust and an increased rate of breaches of trust to a final splitting of the group. Though they are rife between all degrees of relatives, field observations seem to indicate that they are more easily controlled, the closer the agnatic relationship. This is consistent with kinship values (cf. pp. 40 ff.); on this level I shall assume that such values guide the behavior and the degree of trust between close kinsmen. Between such persons, a clear distribution of authority will also facilitate cooperation and sharing and the settlement of petty disputes. Thus, as between father and sons and similarly between senior and junior full brothers, these difficulties can usually be controlled. Increasingly, between agnatic half-brothers, uncle and nephew, and cousins, mutual distrust will increase and the controls on conflict will be weakened, so the probability of a division of the joint herd will increase with collateral distance.

Such a division will probably lead initially to segmentation but not to fission of the camp, and the pattern of herd-owning segments within a camp will thus tend to be consistent with the descent charter of the group. However, when splits do occur between very closely related persons, one may expect the conflict to create greater bitterness, leading to the departure from camp of one of the contending parties. Such close agnates will furthermore not be able to rally factions that will be consistent with the descent segmentation, so the effects of these conflicts will be to disturb the identity between camp/herd-group membership and descent position.

In other words, difficulties over sharing will lead to a progressive internal segmentation of growing camps into independent herd-owning units that tend to correspond to descent segments, but occasionally they will also lead to alienation of very close agnates and the departure from camp of some such agnates.

(ii) Disagreements over joint migration policy, on the other hand, will mainly divide the herd-owning segments of the camp, since they are the units that pursue such policies, while joint owners are once removed from the option of pursuing independent policies. The systematic considerations that might lead to differing migration policies between segments are those of size of herds and complement of personnel in domestic groups, with associated pattern of subsistence. Equal division of inheritance between collaterals might lead segments on the whole to have relatively similar interests, at least initially; otherwise there is nothing in the model so far to suggest any greater tendency for close than for distant collateral herd-owning segments to stay together in camp.

The positive ties that connect a herd-owning unit to any particular camp would seem to be very weak indeed. Thus one would expect progressive alienation and eventual separation of different herd-owning units into separate and independent camps. Such camps would contain a preponderance of close agnates, and increase by natural growth and division will constantly produce predominantly agnatic descent segments as the nuclei of camps.

(iii) The fear of adultery is a third factor leading to fission. Its importance can be appreciated only against the background of the discussion of the topic in Chapter V, showing the value placed on extra-marital love in Marri life. A man desperately fears the shame of his wife's infidelity, while he strongly desires opportunities for liaisons on his own part. He thus wants membership in a camp in which he can expect his wife to be relatively safe and supervised in his absence; adultery suspicion within a camp is explosively destructive to that camp. Despite occasional assertions to the contrary, one must believe that adultery takes place within as well as between camps (pp. 67 f.), and thus the fear, suspicion, and discovery of it may be judged to be a significant factor in determining the composition and persistence of camps.

This factor may be seen to have a significant selective effect because of the extension of the incest ban among Marri (cf. p. 39). Thus, relations with a FaWi, FaBrWi, BrWi, SoWi, and BrSoWi are regarded as incestuous, and fear of adultery will be directed toward persons outside this group of close agnates. Moreover, the shame of a wife's adultery also reflects on these agnates, so they can be counted on to take a positive interest in defending the husband's rights. In other words, even when close agnates are divided as to herd-ownership, a special relationship of trust will persist between them. They will therefore more readily form camp communities than will men of other independent herd units, and one whole set of disruptive issues is eliminated as a potential source of fission between them.

No similar extension of the incest ban takes place through women; sexual relations between wife's married sister/sister's husband are not incestuous, and cases of such adulterous relations are recorded. However, a wife's kinship position does affect the direction of a husband's fear of adultery, since her close kin, that

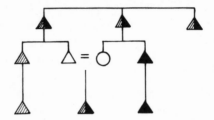

▲   debarred from having relations
    with the woman because of
    consanguinity

▨   debarred from having relations
    with the woman by being her
    husband's agnates.

FIGURE 9

is, WiBr, WiFa, WiFaBr, WiBrSo, cannot be suspected of adultery with her (cf. Fig. 9). A man can thus feel safe about his wife in a camp together with these affines, and some basis for a preferential camp association could thus be argued also for the uxorilocal case. This can be only a weak effect, however, since the relation of trust, in contrast to that between agnates, is not reciprocal: the uxorilocal husband is as great a threat as any other stranger to the wives of other camp members; so no special mutual basis for coresidence exists between affines on this count.

Thus new light is thrown on the role of FaBrDa marriage in furthering camp stability among Marris. Through marriage between such agnates, the safeguards against adultery within a camp that spring from a woman's kinship position are added to those that arise from her affinal position. Most successfully in the form of reciprocal sister exchange, agnatic cousin marriage draws the collateral agnates back into the field controlled by the incest ban; thereby the group of men between whom trust and easy camp coresidence can be maintained is nearly doubled. In other words, camps in which the members are closely related through agnatic cousin marriages can be expected to be more stable, since dissensions caused by suspicion of adultery are less likely to arise. Moreover, the members of such camps are more free to communicate and work effectively with one another without having to observe the restrictions and avoidances of non-kin. The Marri concept of *wati* ("close relative") seems to be primarily an expression for this kind of intimate trust and unity and thus denotes a circle of kin that arises as the result of the several independent factors of agnatic and cognatic relation, marriage pattern, and habitual coresidence, with the consequent absence of threats to stability and mutual trust in domestic life.

(iv) Finally, competition for formal leadership in a camp is a fourth major factor that may lead to fission. The cultural necessity among Marris of having such a formal leadership position, even for the smallest group, has been discussed above (p. 73), as have the features of etiquette that give emphasis and prominence to the leader's position. Apparently, many men aspire to this position, the lowest of stable leadership positions in society, and, further, the principles of ascription are such that rival pretenders will tend to be the closest of agnates.

Unlike the other factors leading to fission, which tend to correlate positively with agnatic distance, the leadership factor strikes at the core of the agnatic group. Tension, opposition, and finally overt rivalry tend to develop between a leader and his successor and between persons with differing claims to the position, thus characteristically between father and senior son, father's brother and deceased senior brother's son, and agnatic half-brothers. Once overt rivalry has developed, the joint camp cannot long be sustained as a single unit, and the two contenders will separate, each with his own following. These followings cannot correspond to agnatic segments, since the contenders tend to be close agnates; their competing appeal to followers cannot be based on agnatic closeness but must depend on other factors, such as parallel interests in terms of size of capital and labor force, or complementary relations of employment and service, or matrilateral or personal relations. As a result, a situation will be produced in which descent segments are split: the close agnates of every person tend to be distributed among two or three camps, while some more-distant agnates will remain coresident with him. Between these more distant agnates in the camp factors [ii] and [iii] above will tend to produce progressive alienation. But, until the depleted group of close agnates grows to a size sufficient to form a camp of its own, the positive factors of mutual need for cooperation and defense will tend in the direction of keeping even relatively distant agnates together.

The balance of strength between these fissive factors and the factors holding persons together in a camp will vary with certain critical external circumstances that determine the minimal and optimal sizes of camps. Thus the number and variety of livestock owned by the group will affect its labor needs, while the age and sex composition of families will affect the number of independent house-holds that are required to make up this minimal labor force. However, when the alienation of kinsmen and coresidents in a camp reaches such a pitch that sep-aration is virtually necessary, the option of bringing in a complete stranger on a shepherding contract is always present. Thus one is never fully committed to coreside with any particular kind of kinsman, though the strong dislike of having strangers in a camp will serve as an important brake on premature fission.

Second, the minimal and optimal size of camps will also be affected by the external circumstances of security. Thus camps migrating in Pathan areas, and to a less extent those traveling widely in the Marri area, will need to be bigger than those moving in the more restricted perimeter of a home area. However, these restrictions are not absolute; they will serve as a brake but not as a ban on fission. Thus a camp, even under the stress of living in the Pathan area, may choose to run the risk of being somewhat too small rather than put up with undesirable company. Because of the division of agnatic groups among several camps, persons will also usually have the option of joining another group of relatives in the case of a split. Finally, the migratory pattern itself can be ad-justed to reduce the risks involved if the camp's size and composition make it desirable. Explicit reference was commonly made to this factor in discussions of migration policy.

In the background there is also an ecologic factor that one, for the sake of completeness, should not forget: an upper limit is imposed on the desirable size of camp by scarce and scattered water resources, poor grazing, etc. Apparently this limit is rarely approached, and the social factors leading to fission are effec-tive before the ecologic pressure makes itself felt. In this sense one may say that the social form produced by the combination of organizational and valuational features is adaptive to a subsistence and environment in which a fragmentation and dispersal of the population is advantageous.

If the factors summarized in this model are the ones that most significantly determine camp size and composition, one should be able to explain the range of forms recorded in the field by the help of these factors. Charts I and II sum-marize this variety of forms. The camps are ordered in terms of the circum-stances to which they are subject. Thus, group A includes those in which size is not particularly encouraged: poor camps that move within a restricted perim-eter in the Marri area. These camps tend to be more short-lived (A1 no longer existed in 1960); the main ties that may permit them to develop to any size and have greater stability over time are those of agnatic cousin marriage (A2).

With greater wealth (B1–B3), camps should tend to be larger. Such an in-creased size may be based both on agnatic coresidence and on shepherd con-

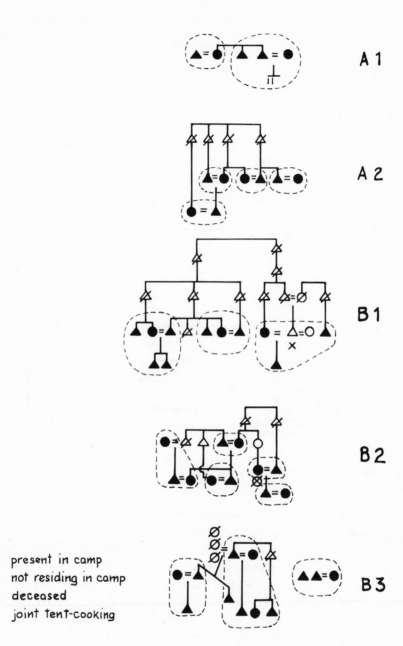

A 1

A 2

B 1

B 2

B 3

▲ present in camp
△ not residing in camp
⚠ deceased
⬭ joint tent-cooking

CHART I

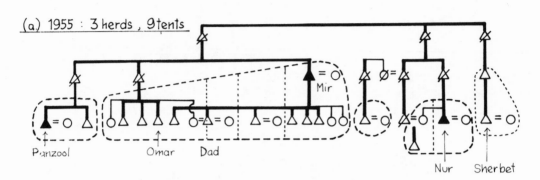

joint herd
joint tent-cooking
▲ *master of the herd*

(names are fictitious)

(a) 1955 : 3 herds , 9 tents

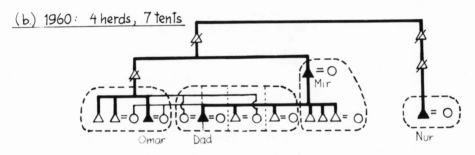

(b) 1960 : 4 herds, 7 tents

CHART II. Camp C

tracts, when agnates cannot or do not wish to form a cooperating group of the
size required to herd the animals. These contracts are made by the wealthy core
of the camp with their distant agnates (B1—shepherds of a wealthy clan chief,
marked *x*, himself not resident in the camp but represented by a non-favorite
wife and their son), or with close matrikin (B2), or with strangers (B3—two
unrelated full-time shepherds in a joint household). Again, the effects of agnatic
endogamy in delaying fission may be seen in camp B2.

Camp C (Chart II) depicts the situation in which size is most encouraged:
relatively wealthy camps migrating under conditions of external insecurity in
Pathan areas. Here clusters of agnates remain together to form larger camps;
however, these camps in no way constitute lineage segments, since their membership includes far from all close agnates. Thus, though both the external threat
and the need for economic cooperation constitute brakes on fission, internal con-

flicts still mount up, and the separation of antagonists takes place. When such rifts develop between wealthy collaterals, each faction will form its own independent camp, and camp size must be maintained through shepherd contracts or defensive coresidence with matrikin or distant agnatic relatives.

A more detailed account of the development of camp C over the last generation illustrates a number of the factors emphasized in the model. The core of the camp in about 1930 consisted of three married brothers, the senior one serving as camp leader after the death of their father. There probably were also peripheral members of the camp, but they cannot be exactly identified. Shortly after, the camp leader died. The next brother in line succeeded to camp leadership and sons were born to both surviving brothers, making the picture, by about 1945, as in Chart III, (a).

At this point Baba died and Mir became leader of the camp. Mir achieved the position because Razool, the senior son of the senior brother, was still relatively young and was, besides, regarded by many as being lazy and worthless. Nonetheless, opposition between Mir and Razool started to mount and finally came to a head over the disposal of certain lands held jointly by the descent group. Razool wished to sell because he needed money, but Mir refused. Razool

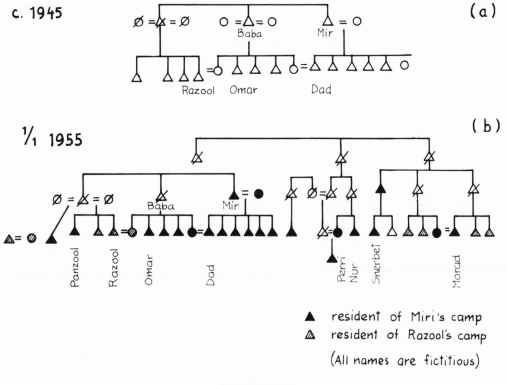

CHART III

broke away and established an independent camp, taking one of his brothers and some more distant collaterals with him.

By the winter of 1955, the composition of the two camps was as in Chart III, (b), which omits some unimportant females and female relationships. The two camps migrated close to each other, since Razool's camp was not yet of a size to defend itself adequately. Panzool, who had his unmarried half-brother living with him, tended to shift between Mir's and Razool's camps as opportunities and grievances dictated. Early in the year, Morad, who had been serving as shepherd for Panzool, was fetched by his brothers and made to join Razool's camp. Though the rift between the two camps was minimized by Mir, and numerous marriage ties also connected them and made for intimate and free contact, there was no doubt that Razool was seeking to establish full independence and equality.

The next issue to develop, during the summer of 1955, was connected with the segmentation between Baba's descendants and Mir and his descendants. Until then they had all herded jointly, Mir acting as guardian for his deceased brother's children (cf. Chart II, a). In this capacity he held disposal over three kinds of vital resources: labor, animals, and marriageable girls.

As for the first, he explained the advantages of the division of labor to Omar: "We plow and reap. You herd." Thus Omar was set to herd the sheep, his youngest brother the lambs, while the smallest did not yet work. Mir's smallest son also stayed at home, the next son looked after the kids, the next the goats, and two full-grown sons were free to do agricultural work wherever tenancy contracts were advantageous, regardless of the location of the camp. The eldest son, Dad, remained in camp as assistant camp leader. Omar, however, being the eldest of a group of brothers, wished to exercise independent authority.

With respect to animals, Omar and his brothers' share of the joint flock, especially when counted per capita, was greater than that of Mir and his sons. Thus he felt that he and his brothers were constantly losing on the joint arrangement. This was acknowledged in principle by Mir: "Now you are mature, it is time for you to take your share. Before, you were immature and we ate and profited in one place. Now it is time for us to go two ways."

However, the issue of marriageable girls and the need for wives for the unmarried men was most critical. To be recognized as mature, Omar must get married. Once recognized as mature it would shortly become his responsibility to provide a wife for his next-in-line brother. Mir, on the other hand, with four unmarried sons and only two daughters of his own, was eager to make an arrangement while he still had disposal, as guardian, of Omar's two sisters. Their disposal was under the constraint of Baba's deathbed wish that he wanted all his children to be married to Mir's children. However, before his death he had made an exchange gamble that had turned out very successfully for his own children; he had given his eldest daughter in marriage to Mir's son Dad, in return for the promise of the then-very-young daughter of Mir for his own son Omar *and* the promise of any future daughter of Mir for his second son. Such a girl was shortly born, and thus both Mir's daughters, as of 1955, were already promised in payment for Dad's long-consummated marriage—leaving Mir neither daughters nor sufficient animals to exchange for wives for his sons, once Omar became independent.

These issues all came to a head with Omar's demand for a division of the herd. "As long as the animals were together Omar could not make any transactions [involving animals or women] without knowledge and consent from Mir; therefore Mir wanted to make his arrangements while he still had control of Omar's property." Several days of argumentation followed. Mir's wife sat in her tent yelling at Omar's oldest sister, who was also her daughter-in-law and who sat in the adjoining tent thirty yards away: "Now you have wives for your brothers, you don't care that your father and my husband were brothers. Now all you care for is animals and money for your son. You can't get full on my husband's animals!" Finally, agreement was reached that Omar would get his animals and his bride, and his brother would get Mir's last remaining daughter, but that, in return, Mir would get Omar's sister for his eldest unmarried son— against the promise that Omar's youngest brother would get the first daughter born of any of Mir's sons. These final negotiations were held in secret, led for Omar by his eldest sister, who decided on the grounds that "Mir's people are too strong for us, our father is dead, my brothers are young, and Mir's sons [including her own husband] are many. We cannot go off and live by ourselves." Thereupon, the herd was divided and Omar's marriage celebrated.

In the subsequent years (cf. Chart II, *b*) segmentation proceeded further and the camp declined in size despite a healthy natural growth rate. First, the fissive issue of camp leadership arose again, this time between the leader and his successor. In retrospect, the first indications may be seen in 1955. Then Omar and his brothers, as Mir's wards, lived not with Mir but with his eldest son, Dad, as was natural, since Dad's was the tent of their sister and their connection with it was one of dependence for the female services of baking, cooking, and washing. Nonetheless it permitted the opposition to be polarized between Mir's tent and Dad's tent, in the person of the latter's wife. Furthermore, Mir's eldest unmarried (widowed) son chose to take his bread from Dad's tent rather than from that of his father and mother. Finally, in decision-making, the three elder sons often formed a group opposed to Mir and the three younger sons. The position of authority held by Dad was increasingly acknowledged: "There are two leaders in this camp: my husband and my eldest son. The rest of them, they are like sheep grazing on the hillside."

By 1960, the herd had been divided between Mir and his younger sons, on the one side, and the three elder sons, on the other. Dad intermittently pitched his tents far enough away from his father's that his segment of the camp would have its own guest site and he could receive the *hal* greeting himself, as head of that segment.

With the growth and proliferation of households occupied by Mir and his sons, the pressures binding them and their more distant collaterals were relaxed, and thus the brakes on fission were removed. The result was a number of defections. Panzool and his brother (now married but sharing a joint herd with Panzool) moved and joined up permanently with their brother Razool in his camp. By such accretion, and by natural growth, Razool's camp reached a size that made it feel secure on its own, and the special relationship of neighborhood and parallel migration was discontinued between the camps of Razool and Mir.

Several other defections also took place. In 1955 Nur was master of a herd composed of his own animals and those of his widowed sister Perri and her son (his FaBrSoSo and closest male agnate). Frictions were already developing in this relationship of jointness. One evening Mir commented on Nur's generosity to his sister in letting her stay with her son, not selling her into a new marriage, and helping her manage the flock until her son came of age.

"And what does she do in return? She tells her son: 'Look what your mother's brother is doing to you, how he is cheating you of your rightful share of the animals.' The boy himself would be content with my treatment, but she keeps making talk against me, urging him to defend his own rights." "Yes, I can see what will happen in two or three years when either the boy becomes a man or is given a wife and called a man like we did with Omar. They will insist on making shares and Perri will set up a cry to her son, to me, and to you about your cheating your poor orphaned sister's child!"

By 1960 Perri's son was married, the herd divided, and he had moved with his mother to reside in the camp of his affines.

Finally, Sherbet, the last representative of the third main descent segment of the original camp (cf. Chart II, *a*), had moved and joined his own brother, long resident in a third camp different from both Mir's and Razool's.

A number of the major factors of growth and fission are thus illustrated in the development history of camp C. The processes of persistence of that camp, which have determined its changing membership through the years, are clearly numerous and complex, which seems characteristic of Marri camps in general— their composition cannot be adequately described by any single, predominant pattern of membership. The most adequate model by which to analyze the Marri camp is therefore not one that depicts the form of community directly, as might a typology of camps, nor is it one that describes a single dominant pattern of recruitment. Rather, I have chosen to construct a model composed of the various factors that seem most prominently to constrain membership in these communities; it thus consists of a set of components that in various degrees affects people's interest in living together. These components may be visualized as both pushes and pulls. The "pulls" are especially that of jointness in property and experience arising from descent and virilocality of marriage and that of the shared interest arising from the needs for security in numbers and for a division of labor in agriculture and herding a variety of animals. The "pushes" are the common issues that arise among people and lead to alienation or loss of trust and thus are conducive to fission; the most important ones among Marris are difficulties over sharing, disagreement over migration policy, fear of adultery, and competition for leadership. The importance of each of these components varies with the external circumstances in which the persons find themselves. Thus this limited set of components will generate a variety of forms of camps, each understandable from the circumstances that produced it.

In the preceding pages I have tried to show how this model will generate the main varieties of observed camp form under the range of circumstances that characterize Marri nomadic life. I have also sought to show how it will explain the details of development and change within one camp over time. The adequacy of the model thus seems to be supported, for it may be judged to depict the main determinants of camp form among the Marri.

VIII

RELATIONS AMONG CAMPS; THE POSITION
OF THE INDIVIDUAL

"There was once an age when no one told lies, when no one thieved, when no one did wicked things. All the people were good. At that time, leopards and the white bird called the Dodo could talk to people, and they would understand. . . . That age of course has passed. A great earthquake occurred, burying all those good people under the earth. Now we have been born afterward—our people: lying, stealing, doing our evil work."

THE PRECEDING analysis of camp composition has exposed the processes of growth, division, and individual and household mobility in nomadic Marri camps. These processes also have a number of necessary implications for the interrelations between camps, which may serve as the foundation for a sketch of wider social organization. Primarily, they produce a patterned distribution of ties among the members of different communities.

First, a network of kinship relations is woven between camps. From the high frequency of agnatic cousin marriage one might expect an overwhelming concentration of kin within the camp, but, because of the small size of the camps and the higher frequency of other forms of mobility, a dispersal of kin ties is in fact effected. Fission leads to the subdivision of a descent group into several camps. Despite this division, however, agnatic endogamy tends to continue within the descent group, and thus a small cluster of camps will be related, both by being composed largely of members of the same descent group of three or four generations' depth and by close matrilateral kinship. Most individual and household mobility will continue to take place among camps so related, maintaining the cluster for at least some generations. But in most camps there are also members of other agnatic groups; each descent segment seems to have a history of intermarriage and occasional residential interchange of male members with a couple of other similar descent segments. In the case of the two camps illustrated on page 95, who are predominantly Gawarani, such a relationship connects them with the Mitiani and Siahozai—descent groups of different branches of the same major section (Powadhi) of the Marri tribe (cf. Appendix I).

The ties among the camps of a cluster are also given ceremonial expression. The occasions for this expression are mainly the rites of passage of camp mem-

100

bers: birth, betrothal, marriage, funeral, and mortuary commemoration. At such times the household directly concerned gives a feast (*hairat*), and the members of the camps of the cluster are invited—either all, as for the major communal feasts, or only those of the appropriate sex. Indeed, everyone cannot come, since the herds and tents cannot be left unguarded, but those who appear do so as the representatives of their camp, and will arrive in a body to mark their collective status. An exemplification of this ceremonial behavior is given in Appendix III. Groups of men and boys from a camp may also make such collective appearances in another camp of the cluster during slack periods for mere amusement, when the visitors and the hosts, respectively, will form teams for playing

Winter hut to which a camp regularly returns. Groups that own such winter huts refer to their location as "our homeland."

or gambling against each other, on penalty of collective mock punishment or fine.

The agnatic ties of camp members from other descent groups, and the maternal links deriving from the proportion of non-endogamous marriages, provide a wider net of relations to camps more loosely connected than those within the cluster but potentially cultivable through further intermarriage and coresidence to the extent that in time they could become more important.

Camps migrating in Marri area and cultivating their own lineage-owned lands will readily retain their section and subsection or descent identity despite such intermixing. For the large number of camps that spend much time in Pathan country and do agriculture on a tenancy basis, if at all, this anchoring in a joint estate is lacking, and for them the foregoing description may have overemphasized the descent segment as a unit of reference. In their case there should be nothing to prevent compound camps from changing their main constitution from being predominantly of one descent segment to being predominantly of another, without any noticeable realignment. But this intermingling can readily take place only among groups practicing allegiance to the same section chief.

There is one other set of personal ties that connects camps and affects their relation to one another: the illicit liaisons between lovers. Migration policy and routes are modified by the influential men to bring their camp close to the camps of mistresses, and junior members also try through intermediaries to effect adjacent camping and parallel migration. A man will often intrigue to have a camp member establish a contract to employ as shepherd the husband of his mistress, and women also discreetly try to influence their husbands, brothers, and sons to lead the camp in the direction of their lovers. However, it would appear that this set of adulterous relations develops mainly between persons in camps already connected with each other and so will tend to reinforce the existing contacts among camps in one cluster and among more tenuously related camps, rather than change the existing patterns.

There are thus numerous factors that combine to produce a tendency for clusters of camps to form—an inner core of one or two closely related camps and an outer fringe of more loosely connected, "friendly" camps. The inner core will be contained within the larger category of the following of a section chief and has a predominant descent unity; the wider circle is one of more tenuous kinship, acquaintance, and adulterous adventure. This outer circle is also the one within which labor will generally be exchanged through contract and vicarious security can be obtained through aggregation. For the daily life of commoners, these two degrees of camp association are without a doubt more important than is the segmentary charter of tribal sections and subsections or the echelons of leaders and their political followings.

Beyond this wider circle of camps, again, Marris have use for contacts and acquaintances. They need the host-and-trader partners (*bradir*) in villages, and they need contacts with other sedentary people to obtain tenancy contracts on land. Most importantly, they need contacts to obtain news and information about pastures, the movements of other camps, tribal matters, and intertribal relations. Much of this news passes by means of the customary *hal* greetings, and though not always adequately informative the news communicated through *hal* is nonetheless eagerly sought by all. However, the institutional form of *hal* makes it difficult actively to solicit news by means of it: the initiator is at a disadvantage, since his is the obligation to speak and inform and explain fully, while the host is allowed to be far more reticent in the information he gives. Thus Marris are not encouraged to seek contact with strangers outside the circle in which all are well known to each other and in which they can expect a modicum of co-operation and truthfulness (cf. the informant statement, Chap. IV, p. 46). And, even within this circle, relations are highly ambivalent. Members of different camps compete for grazing, for water, and for tenancy contracts. They fear theft and deception; they suspect adulterous intentions; in short, they expect trouble to arise even from contact with closely related people. There is thus an incentive to keep the circle of participation narrow, to limit the number of camps and persons falling within the committing categories of relationship, and to limit the number of occasions for contact even with them. Therefore, camps are hidden away so that travelers will not see and find them, and on the occasions when others pitch their camp even moderately close to a previously settled camp, the intruders will be roundly cursed. On migration, one day, informants commented: "Now where we are going there will be many camps, many Marris. . . . If they are kinsfolk (*azziz*), then it is good; if they are strangers (*seyyal*), then it is bad." "No, it's not good in either case, living close together."

Despite each individual's clear position in a ramifying system of descent groups and sections, in a centralized pyramidal political organization of echelons of leaders and their followings, and in a multifarious network of dyadic relations of kinship, acquaintances, liaisons, and contracts, the final resultant organization is thus one that encapsulates him rather completely in a small, residential community maintaining only a few strands of regular interaction within a narrow circle of similar camps. This situation comes about mainly by a strong involuting tendency with respect to all non-ascriptive relationships and by a number of controls on the occasions and desirability of interaction with persons outside the camp.

Clearly, this situation has a significant feedback effect on political life. A rather unsatisfactory analysis of the formal tribal political organization was given in Chapter III, which failed to answer questions of why such a political form has developed and why people put up with it. In part, these are naïve forms of basically historical questions; the present Marri organization is a system radically modified by recent changes in the external environment (the organization and flow of trade, the forms of wealth, the nature of administration in adjoining areas) and by active interference from the colonial power. There is much evidence to suggest that, when the main formal outlines of Marri tribal organization were created, the chiefs or nobles functioned essentially as warrior leaders in an anarchic area adjoining major caravan routes. They thus served to organize a marginal mixed farming and herding population for purposes of raiding and looting, and one can see in present Marri camp life the institutions of free contract based on agreed systems of sharing that would give substance to such an organization, in which the profit incentives were strong. The system of *jirga* councils and the echelons of leaders would then have been an organ of coordination between such warrior leaders to reduce internal strife and facilitate joint action in defense and, occasionally, in large-scale conquest of strategic land areas.

In this century, through the agency of a colonial administration practicing indirect rule, this formal organization has been misinterpreted or purposely re-formed or at any rate transformed into what is essentially a system of native courts supported in their decisions by external force. The factor of contract and consent from below hardly enters any more in the way that it must have when the organization was tested in battles for survival and loot. In the new situation effective controls from below on the leaders can be exercised only if there is a development of local parties or factions and an active public opinion among commoners, which could lead to concerted action from followers in support of, or defection from, rival leaders. With a pattern of camp and intercamp organ-ization such as that described above, it should be clear that no such factions can develop. Thus those born into positions of privilege, and the few reckless, tough, and talented persons who dare and manage to assert leadership on a level higher than the individual camp, cannot be controlled or contained from below. With-drawal, dispersal, servility, and deceit become the only means of defense for the commoners. As seen from the tent camp, then, the tribal leaders belong to an-other world, one with which commoners have contact through *jirga* court cases and taxation demands and through occasionally being cuckolded by a nobleman, but which does not seem to grow out of the life and institutions of their own communities.

"Our section chief is a brave and manly person, but he does nothing for us, just robs us of our valuables. We cannot go to other chiefs because they rule different sections, and our section chief's brother just passes us on back to him. Nor will the Tahsildar do anything for us—if he hears we are here [in Pathan country], he just comes to collect the grazing tax or chase us away. The supreme chief does nothing for us either; he rarely comes to Marri area at all, but at least he does not fleece us extra, as did his predecessor, who went around extorting 20 rupees here and 100 rupees there and a sheep a third place."

This distrust, leading to a relative dissociation from collectivities and group commitments, is a general feature of Marri life. As a rule of behavior, it is summed up in the Marri concept of *taggi* ("deceit," silence about truth and im-portant matters). Associated with the practice of *taggi* is also the importance attached to secrecy (*likainagh/israri*), which is an actor's best protection against interference or exploitation. The same patterns assert themselves in a number of domains of behavior; whether as the ultimate effect of the Marri system of organization or as its root cause, the practice of *taggi* and the forms of Marri social organization are intimately connected.

It should be emphasized that the practice of *taggi* in no way implies a failure in the culture to develop clear rules of conduct and directives about the mutual obligations of partners in a relationship. In ethical terms, the Marri distinguish between two realms: that of *haqq* ("duty or obligation") and that of *jind-i-marzie* ("own will, inclination"). Under the first fall such things as basic custom law (*riwaj*) and the commandments of Islam, as understood by Marris. One informant, in enumerating the five pillars of Islam, went on to say: "The Prophet also said that man should not tell lies, should refrain from evil. . . ." But he was contradicted by others present: "No, lying or telling the truth or doing evil or doing good—that doesn't matter. If a man does those five things you have enumerated, then his duties to God are fulfilled. Whether he thieves, tells lies, etc.—that only pertains to his own *namuz* [name = honor]."

The non-duty realm, then, is the realm of acts that bring merit, honor, or shame; it encompasses a number of the basic values of Marri culture, many of which can also be clearly verbalized by Marri informants. The difficulty is that they do not add up to consistent directives for behavior in concrete situations. He who fulfils his *haqq* scrupulously is a fool (*ganookh*), to be taken advantage of; he who breaks it may be sued before the *jirga* court. He who takes no mistress is unmanly and unworthy of admiration; he who does may be killed without recompense. In such a situation, actors will be encouraged to pursue their various goals in a carefully circumspect manner, and the control over information about one's self is essential. The essential role of *taggi*, or the practice of secrecy and deceit by the individual, can then be readily understood; it allows persons to pursue disparate aims and maintain social relations on contradictory and incompatible bases.

Social implications of *taggi* have been emphasized throughout the preceding analysis. When practiced knowingly by the members of a community, its structural effects are profound. In a situation in which each person suspects his neighbor of opportunistically pursuing disparate ends, and the expectation of *taggi* absolves him even from needing evidence to nurture his suspicion, social organization must to an extreme degree be reduced to an individual and dyadic, rather than a corporate, level. There is a failure to develop binding commitments that would make aspects of a person inseparable from a larger collectivity or corporate group—what a person will do in a specific instance is more directly determined by the valued goods he can obtain than by the obligations of his relationship to his *alter* at the moment. Such lack of trust leads to the consolidation of the *individual* as the basic unit of social organization—larger collectivities are precarious, depend on tactically adequate means of mutual control, and do not regulate behavior outside their field of avowed purpose and effective sanction.

This basic structural feature of Marri society may also be traced in the forms of religious and ritual practices. There is no poverty of symbolic expression in Marri culture, and various such idioms and expressions have been noted in con-

nection with the preceding analysis of social life. But no sustained analysis of
ritual or religion has been attempted, and no correspondences between secular
social groupings and what might be described as cult groups have been found.
I suggest that this is not entirely an artifact of incomplete data, but rather another implication of the non-corporate bases of Marri social life. The consistency
of the material from this point of view is notable.

Marris are widely reported to be "lax" Mohammedans, as they themselves will
be the first to agree. In fact, Islam provides some very basic and moving idioms
for the expression of corporate unity, especially in the collective prayers facing
Mecca, in the Friday meeting, and in the communal fast. Such idioms are prominently utilized by neighboring Pathans, partly under similar ecologic circumstances. Marris, however, rarely pray and dismiss the need for so doing by
claiming that their chiefs pray and fast for them—that is, by referring the cult
activity to the one collectivity that is stable and to the officeholder who is its
organizational kingpin. The Marris who do pray, do so separately, each to save
his separate soul.

The other activities relating to the supernatural are overwhelmingly magic,
spells and incantations concerned with protection; they ward off bad luck, evil
eye, sickness, and spirits. Even when they concern joint property, they are
pursued in a spirit of self-interest and are executed individually. Thus, citing
from Jean Pehrson's notes:

"Each herd is under the protection of a dead saint, living Sayyid, or Allah. The first
lamb every year is given to that person or sacrificed in his name. The goats are under
a different protector. K. K. today took our clean brass bowl and filled it with water,
dipping in it a *tavis* [amulet] given by the Sayyid, wrapped in clean white cloth. Then
he sprinkled the water over the backs of the flock. Three had sickened and died and
he did that to prevent further losses."

There is no indication that special relations are established between persons
dependent on the same shrine or Sayyid for such protection. Dough is sacrificed
to the fire before bread-baking when the person baking believes it necessary;
incantations are mumbled privately to ward off bad luck; signs and portents of
individuals' futures are sought in sheep scapulae and breastbones. When a sheep
starts lowing, signaling that death is near, someone may rise and go to slit its
ear with a knife or beat it to make it stop. Thus dangers that may affect or
threaten all are not dealt with by the mobilization of cult groups but by individual actions. Even the practices that might seem to express group adherence—
the distribution of a piece of bread to all other tents in camp when the new
moon is sighted, the distribution of bread and sweets to at least one tent after
a bad dream or on happy life-cycle occasions—make use of idioms that are
generally used in the Middle East to ward off envy and the evil eye and that

Young shepherd with kid.

also here are most readily understood as means of protecting individual interests and successes against such threats.

Thus, most religious and ritual activities seem to be instrumentally directed at sustaining the individual and his separate interests and concerns. Where they fail, the Marri interpret this also through the asocial and amoral concept of fate (*nasib*), which figures prominently in their discourse.

When interpersonal life is so strongly dominated by suspicion and distrust, and the individual emerges so strongly as the unit of organization, it seems necessary to look beyond social relations to find the things that make life tolerable, enjoyable, or exciting to the Marris and that thus serve to give their social life the form it has. In this description and analysis of Marri society, I have mainly attempted to find them in the *goods* that are valued in Marri culture: food, animals, labor services, sexual services, respect, and deference. The pursuit of such ends under ecological and tactical constraints gives, if this analysis is correct, both complexity and meaning to social life and produces the fascinating, flamboyant, gay, and dramatic character that pervades Marri behavior. However, perhaps for this same reason, Marris, more strikingly than the members of most societies, seem to experience a loss of direction and purpose as old age dulls the appetites. Thus one old man, who had succeeded in increasing his flock to a thousand sheep and goats and who had a young wife, a senior son of considerable ability, and several other sons, would repeat the same lament every night as he lay waiting for sleep to come: "Allah Ji, Allah Ji! My heart has gone with Mohammed, peace be upon him; but my body happens to have been left here— a man's empty form. And an old man's form, at that."

REFERENCES CITED

Baluchistan District Gazetteer
1907. Vol. II. Allahabad: Pioneer Press. Vol. III. Bombay: Times Press.

BARTH FREDRIK
1954. "Father's Brother's Daughter Marriage in Kurdistan." *Southwestern Journal of Anthropology*, Vol. X.
1964. "Competition and Symbiosis in North East Baluchistan." *Folk*, Vol. VI.

BRUCE, R. I.
1900. *The Forward Policy and Its Results*. London.

DAMES, M. LONGWORTH
1904. *The Baloch Race*. Asiatic Society Monographs, Vol. IV. London.

DUKE, O. T.
1883. *A Historical and Descriptive Report on the District of Thal Chotiali and Harnai*. Calcutta.

GOODENOUGH, W.
1956. "Componential Analysis and the Study of Meaning." *Language*, Vol. XXXII, No. 1.

PEHRSON, ROBERT N.
1954. "The Lappish Herding Leader: A Structural Analysis." *American Anthropologist*, Vol. LVI, No. 6.
1957. *The Bilateral Network of Social Relations in Könkämä Lapp District*. Indiana University Publications, Slavic and East European Series, Vol. V (1957). Reprinted as Vol. VII of *Samiske Samlinger*. Oslo, 1964.

CHART OF MARRI SEGMENTS AND THEIR LEADERS

Based on Kohlu Tahsil records, 1940
(Possibly incomplete for the Ghazeni section)

GHAZENI			
	BAHAWALANZAI	DODAZAI	
	Sardar	DOSTALIZAI	
		MEHRAZAI	
	NOZBANDAGANI	RAHZENZAI	
	Rahzen	JAFOZAI	
		WADERAZAI	BAIKANZAI
			WADERAZAI
		PAHKANZAI	PAHNKANZAI
			GHEVEZAI
			MORALZAI
	MURGIANI	HOTANZAI	
		Sobha	
		Khudadad	
		HODI	
		Roshan	
	SAMWANI		
	Dalu Khan		
	LODHIANI		
	Tal Khan		
	ALIANI	KHURASANI	
	W. Malikdad Khan	Alihan	
		KHATRANI	
		Malho	
		ALIZAI	
		Mirzihan	
		KOHECHI	
		Durehan	
	ISPANI	BALACHANI	
	Mir Mohammed Khan	Maskef	
		DUREHANZAI	
		Malho	
		SHAHDADZAI	
		Mir Mohammed Khan	
	LANGHANI	MALGHANI	
	W. Mahmud Khan	Jahmud	
		MULANI-SINDHI	
		Karimdad Khan	

		Mir Faiz Mohammed Khan
		KAISRANI
		Miro Khan
		Mohammed Akbar
		LONDWANI
		Haji Monjan Khan
		CHAKRANI
		Chakar
		JAMANI
		Ghazi Khan
		HEZHWANI
		Faujali
	TINGIANI	
	MAZARANI	
BIJARANI	**KALANDRANI**	**NIHALANZAI**
W. Shah Murad	Tohr Khan	Tohr Khan
M. Tohr Khan	Jabarkhan	Fateh Khan
M. Mir Fateh Khan		**BARANZAI**
		Shah Murad Khan
	KAISRANI	
	Alisher	
	Alihan	
	Ali Khan	
	RAHMKANI	**LALWANI**
	Gula Khan	Durmond
		BIROHI
		Jabar
		Shah Murad
		DARKANI
		Dadhan
		Dalan
		KHAROTANI
		Manghan
		DALRAHMKANI
		Gula Khan
	PIRADANI-MARRI	**SHALOZAI**
	Haji Dadhan	Jalamb
		FATEHANI
		Ahmed Khan
		KAIMANI
		Tal Khan
	SALARANI	
	Bijar	
	Mando	
	Sabzal	
	SOMRANI	**DAULATANIZAI**
	Mian Khan	Khanum
	Bahar Khan	**SOMRANI**
		Haji
		Hude
		Lalu
		BUDAZAI
		Sahaq

	SHADIHANZAI	
	Gulzar Khan	
	Mian Khan	
KALWANI	**PIRIZAI**	
W. Baghikhan	Kaisar	
	Jamun	
	DAHIZAI	
	Mughalhan	
	KODIANI	
	Paindkhan	
	GIRANI	
	Jamur	
SHAHEJA	**LALUZAI**	
W. Hezho	Jamal	
	NAMBEZAI	
	Tagia	
	SAIDANI	
	Jalan	
	KHURASANI	
	Ghulam Mohammed	
POWADHI	**DEWAZAI**	
Samand Khan	Dewa Khan	
	Sahib Khan	
	MURIDANI	
	Murad Khan	
	KHUDANI	
	Dawala	
	BAJANI	
	Umar	
	MALANGANI	
	Jetha	
	SAHOZAI	
	Khatol	
	DARANRI	
	Moro	
	MANDWANI	
	Dura	
	MITIANI	
	Painti	
	MIANRI	**LINDANRI**
	Miro Khan	Ali Beg
		DAULATANI
		Musa
		SOBHANI
		Miro Khan
		GAUWARANI
		Miskali
		DADWANI
		Baloch
KUNGRANI	**WANECHI**	
W. Yar Mohammed	Wali Mohammed	
Khan		
Kungar Khan	**SHUKLANI**	
	Hazar Khan	

		ISFANI Miskan **HASOZAI** Yar Mohammed Khan Mohammed	
LOHARANI W. Miah Khan M. Samand Khan	**LOHARANI**	**JALAMBANI** Paindkhan **KANRANI** Hotak **GOSRANI** Shadin **SOMRANI** Dawali	
	MOHAMADANI Jadakhan Jhandakhan	**KAWANI** Alokhan **HOTIANI** Amirkhan **SHEHANI** Chhuta Dostin **KAMBIRANI** Nazekhan	
	SHERANI Wazirhan	**SARANGANI** Jalakhan	**BAROHANZAI** Kuneri **SIAHPADH** Jara **HEMDANI** Saleh **RINDKANI** Dalosh **SHUKLANI** Umar **QAWELANI** Shahali
		JANDWANI Shade **MAHLOR & BANGWAR** Wazirhan **DURKANI** Jamalhan	**WALIDADANI** Mirjan

MARRI SARDARS AND THEIR INTERRELATIONS

Extracted from a complete genealogy of the Sardar's male
agnates as collected from his *munshi*

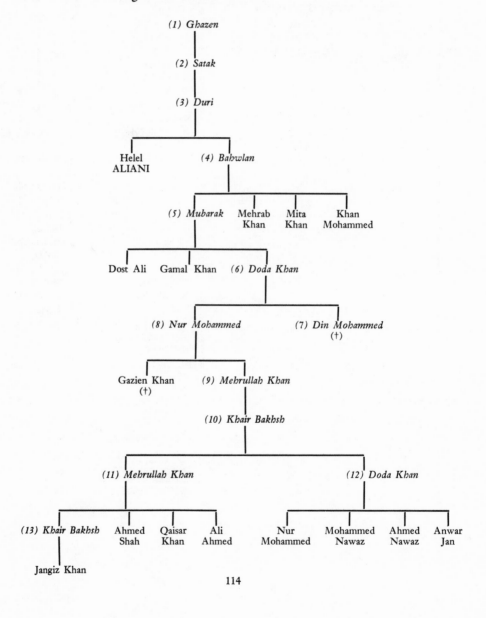

114

A DESCRIPTION OF A BETROTHAL
AND A WEDDING CEREMONY

The betrothal ceremony described below is from a village, in which the prospective groom A is younger brother (father deceased) of one of the two leaders, the prospective bride the daughter of a Brahui of relatively prominent family who are agnates of a family resident in the village. There are tremendous dissensions within A's lineage, and particularly between his brothers and their agnatic cousins. "Our brothers are being married to strangers (*seyyal*), our sisters to relatives (*wati*). We want to marry a stranger, not a relative. We do not like our relatives. They quarrel with us." Previous attempts had been made to get the daughter of C, the other major leader of the village, belonging to another lineage segment (five to six generations removed from the common ancestor). They had been rebuffed. Various informal contacts had been made with the heads of the Brahui girl's household prior to the formal betrothal visit.

A's senior brother was away, and the groom's delegation was composed of his second brother, B, various villagers of the groom's section, four men of the Bahawalanzai (sardar's) section, one saint, altogether twelve men led by C. They gathered in A and B's guestroom and proceeded in a body to the Brahui compound. There they exchanged formal greetings, and C gave the formal news (*hal*), saying that they had heard the girl was good and asking which daughter it was. She was identified as the middle daughter—the elder, unattractive, is not yet married. The Brahuis responded in formal style, accepting the proposal. There were conversations about the bride-price. Then the groom's brother B took over, asking the saint to say prayers. One of the delegation shot off a rifle and was told by B to buy and pass out sweets to the assembled throng. Then B gave Rs. 1,000 as a "tip" (*bakshish*) to the Brahui headman, who gave it to the girl's FaBr (her Fa being insane)—"since *bakshish* is used by the extended family, that's better than bride-price (*lab*), which is against Shariat, can be recovered, and is the exclusive property of the girl's father or his heirs." (This sophistication is unknown to Marri tent-dwellers, who treat *lab* in the way *bakshish* is here characterized.) The atmosphere was formal but friendly, with a clear differentiation and juxtaposition of the two groups of agnates. The visitors were thereupon invited to tea and dinner, paid for by the hosts from Rs. 300

given by A's senior brother for food money. After eating, the groom's delegation quickly left.

Meanwhile, there was a meeting of A's mother, accompanied by Jean Pehrson (other female relatives of A could also have accompanied her), with the girl and her female relatives. Each set of women were dressed in their finest. The girl sat in a corner on a pad of quilt, with her back to the room and covered with a big sari. Formal greetings were given and received by A's Mo and by the highest-ranking Brahui woman (the sister of the chief). The girl's mother brought tea, and A's mother said she did not drink tea at that time of day; otherwise, the two women did not speak, and the silence was subsequently commented on favorably by A's mother. She sat with her sari half-covering her face, being called out occasionally for consultation with her son B. The Brahui women said J. P. must go and sit facing the bride, where her younger sister and cousin had been until then (this was permitted because J. P. was a stranger—a relative of the prospective groom could not sit there). They struggled to pull off the girl's sari so that J. P. could see her—she sat with her eyes downcast and did not speak during the whole time. When given tea, she drank half a cup and cried. Meanwhile her relatives brought drums, sang some, and did a little bit of dancing. Then the rifleshot was heard, and the girl sobbed audibly. Food was then brought, and the two guests ate, none of the hosts joining. After eating, the guests left abruptly, returning to A and B's guestroom. There A's close kin cross-questioned them on what the girl had looked like, about features in detail, and whom in the village was she more or less beautiful than. Even A's mother had not been able to see her face well. A's kinsfolk agreed that the other family had shown the proper amount of modesty (shak) but had been stingy with the food.

The wedding ceremony described below is from a tent camp where betrothal and wedding followed rapidly, precipitated by an orphaned boy's demand for a separation of the herd and for his FaBr and guardian's daughter in marriage, as requested by his Fa on his deathbed.

The day before the wedding was one of rest and preparation. In the evening the kinsfolk put henna on their hands. "We put it on the night before because in the day we must work—at night it will dry." The bride cried a little when told that tomorrow would be her wedding day. 15:30: Animals slaughtered, for combined wedding and Id (calendrical festival). Number of animals: bride's SiHu; also FaBrSo of bride and groom: 1 wedding 1 Id sacrifice. Pehrson (bride's marriage brother): 1 wedding 1 Id sacrifice. Id sacrifices: bride's Fa: 1, groom: 1, bride's other marriage brother: 1, two other camp members: 1 each. The groom sacrificed his wedding animals some days later when he took his wife to his tent. The bride's mother sacrificed one of her own few animals after the legally binding marriage formula was said.

06:30: Two boys about fourteen years of age were given their first pair of pants, having worn the long shirt of childhood until then. They put them on;

the men of the camp caught and held them, threatening to tear their pants off, until all were given a sweet apiece.

06:45: Eldest brother of the bride, Robert Pehrson, and visiting section leader exchanged turbans.

07:00: Shares of candy were made so the shepherds would get theirs before leaving for the day. Substitute shepherds, predominantly women, went out so all close kin of bride and groom could be present. Marriage brothers went to the bride's tent to be served bread, butter, and stew by her mother and her.

10:00: Men and women of a closely related camp arrived for the feast. There was a mock battle by men, firing blank cartridges at each other, and the host women went out and threw water and flour on the arrivals, but everyone was disappointed at the small scale of the fight. The women cried briefly with the bride, then started working on her red wedding dress (normal dress: white), which had been cut by her Mo and HuSi from material furnished by the groom's family. They also provided oil with which the bride's hair was rubbed and combed. Wedding clothes were put on her by her mother, who said: "To what strange camp are you going, that you should weep, my daughter?" and then she herself wept—"For a daughter there is no way to stay with her father and mother." By putting on the dress, the girl becomes a bride (*wani*), and the younger close kinswomen moved up around her to fend off the men who tried to peek at the bride, while she sat bent over, head down, covered completely by her sari, which was held down at the corners by the women. They had sticks with which they hit the boys who approached close; the boys brought dwarf-palm fronds with which to fight back and almost tore the sari at one point. The bride is not shown to her HuSi (her own FaBrDa and BrWi) or to unrelated women of the camp. Nor to any male other than her marriage brother unless a payment (*waspern*) is made, which the marriage brother collects and which becomes the bride's property.

11:00: Men and women, separately, ate, conversed, and slept some, as the day was hot. 13:00: The men started dancing and danced continuously for 45 minutes. Then they had a long barefoot race. 14:00: Target shooting. The bride's Br was sent on horseback to fetch a mullah, but he turned out not to be available, so the wedding ceremony was postponed one day. 17:00: Tug of war, stone-throwing, lifting of small children, physical stunts.

18:00: The flock returned, and the substitute shepherds reported that the goats were lost. Immediately, almost all the men left to search for them. R. P., as marriage brother, went to sit and guard the bride. The visiting leader came, exchanged formal greetings, and tried to lift off her veil but was driven away with a stick. He paid one rupee and was given a short peek. He complained about that and, after some haggling, promised a silver nose ring as a gift, after which he took a long, searching, devoted look—as one adoring the Virgin Mary.

In the evening, the young boys danced, and the bride and her sister joined them briefly. The women gathered around and started a separate dance, which they continued for a while but then called out to the boys to come and join them. On the arrival of the adult men who had been searching for the goats, the bride was rushed off under cover of her sari, by order of her HuSi.

Sexual segregation was maintained in the dance for a while, but later broke down as sweethearts and illicit lovers got next to each other, with much whispering and handholding.

Next day, the "mullah"—a Manghi (Pathan) faquir—arrived early with a Pathan companion. The men came back and reported that the whole herd of goats had been found; the guests from the other camp left, the visiting women each receiving a sari from the groom's family, as did also the wives of the marriage brothers and the bride's mother.

In the afternoon, the wedding ceremony proper took place. The people of the camp gathered, forming an inner circle of the persons directly concerned, in clockwise order: the faquir, bride, bride's Mo, groom's Si, groom, one of bride's marriage brothers, bride's father, her other marriage brother. The remaining women of the camp sat behind the women, the men on the other side behind the men. The bride sat with her face uncovered but with her *back* to the circle, facing her younger unmarried sister.

First, a practice run of the formula was made by the faquir, to teach the bride when to answer. He then recited a long verse from the Koran. Thereupon the faquir questioned the maturity of the couple. The bride's Fa first said that she was immature: "They are neither of them sexually mature (*ballugh*). We are just incidentally marrying the children of our own will." Faquir: "Then his elder sister should speak for him, since he is not mature." Bride's fa: "But we have made him mature. The herd has now been separated out, he is now master of his animals and responsible head of his household." Faquir: "Then he can speak for himself. "

The faquir asked the bride's father, in his capacity as groom's senior agnate, the name of the groom, of his father and mother, and whether there was any other boy by that name from parents of those names. He then asked the same about the bride. He then announced the names of the groom, parents, bride, and parents. Did the father give his daughter happily (*kabol*)? To which the father answered "Yes"—this question and answer being repeated three times. Then the groom if he took the girl happily, to which he answered "Yes" thrice; the mother if she gave her daughter happily (thrice), then the (Marri) marriage brother if he gave his sister happily. He answered "Yes," but that the groom's side must give animals and money and a grindstone and dishes to his sister. A visitor (FaBrSo of both spouses) commented "Some marriage brothers even ask for Rs. 5,000." Marriage brother: "You have said it, now I say it myself. Give her Rs. 5,000!" But her father objected: "This is devil's work!" ("he said that because he did not even want a *mock* fight at the wedding of his Da and BrSo").

R. P., as marriage brother, was asked if he gave his sister happily, and said "Yes." The first marriage brother said: "Well, you show me the animals to give her and I shall be happy," and the groom said that he would later. Then the faquir asked for salt ("We often use the heart of a lamb, and I had saved it this time, but a dog stole it"), blessed it, and gave half each to groom and bride. The bride ate hers. Her father scolded the groom for not eating his, for: "The salt is to ensure peace in the home. If you do not eat it there will be no peace in the tent, no peace at the fireside. The two will be as strangers [seyyal], and how can there be peace between strangers?" Then the bride's father asked what part of his sacrifice (hairat) the groom would give to his bride (i.e., as a dowry), but the groom did not reply. Then the people raised their arms, and the faquir led prayers and asked God to make the couple green and their marriage peaceful and fruitful.

Before separating, the marriage brothers were promised to be shown animals, which the bride would receive from the groom. The faquir left after the ceremony, having been given 1 rupee by the marriage brother and later a kid by the bride's father. The male relatives of the bride caught the groom and put a donkey's packsaddle on him. ("Sometimes the groom is beaten with the packsaddle and with the entrails of animals.")

There was a notable lack of tension between the two families and relative complacency on the part of the girl, doubtless connected with the close kinship ties between the parties and the fact that they were of the same camp. Though even the embroidery on the bride's dress was not finished, there were no complaints, except "this wedding was done just without ceremony at all. Just an old faquir. None of the big fighting of the marriage brother against the rest of the company."

For five days the bride continued to sleep in her mother's tent and do her work. On the sixth day the groom fetched his bride (the daj hairat day). In the morning early his Si and her co-wife set up the wedding tent, and then his Si went to the bride's tent to fetch her and her mother, whereupon the three of them went ceremoniously to the new tent. The HuSi distributed sweetened rice, sugar, and sweet tea to the women who congregated to congratulate the new sister-in-law and her tent, serving the bride first of all. Then she brought in a sprig of green twig heavily smeared with the blood of the groom's sacrificial animal, taking care to spill a few drops on the floor as she put it at the front of the tent. The bride and her mother cried a little, her younger sister cried much. For the first few nights thereafter the groom slept with his animals—to keep them from mixing with the herd from which they had just been separated. At no point was there an explicit or implicit marking of the consummation of the marriage.

Index

INDEX